# A SUSSEX GUIDE

# INSPIRING
# SUSSEX
# GARDENERS

LORRAINE HARRISON

INTRODUCED BY
JOHN BROOKES

*Illustrated by*
SARAH YOUNG

SNAKE RIVER PRESS

# SNAKE RIVER PRESS

**Book No 14**
*Books about Sussex for the enthusiast*

Published in 2008 by
SNAKE RIVER PRESS
South Downs Way, Alfriston, Sussex BN26 5XW
**www.snakeriverpress.co.uk**

ISBN 978-1-906022-13-6

This book was conceived, designed and produced by
SNAKE RIVER PRESS

ART DIRECTOR & PUBLISHER *Peter Bridgewater*
EDITORIAL DIRECTOR *Viv Croot*
EDITOR *Robert Yarham*
PAGE MAKEUP *Richard Constable & Chris Morris*
ILLUSTRATOR *Sarah Young*

This book is typeset in Perpetua & Gill Sans,
two fonts designed by Eric Gill

Printed and bound in China

---

### DEDICATION

*For PGB with thanks*

# CONTENTS

FOREWORD . . . . . . . . . . . . . 6

INTRODUCTION . . . . . . . . . . 8

VANESSA BELL &
   LEONARD WOOLF . . . . . . . 12

WILLIAM BORRER . . . . . . . . 17

JOHN BROOKES . . . . . . . . . . 20

JIM BUCKLAND &
   SARAH WAIN . . . . . . . . . . 24

OLIVE J. COCKERELL &
   HELEN NUSSSEY . . . . . . . . 28

J.R.B. EVISON . . . . . . . . . . . 33

WALTER H. GODFREY . . . . . . 36

GRAHAM GOUGH . . . . . . . . 39

ARTHUR HELLYER . . . . . . . . 43

DEREK JARMAN . . . . . . . . . . 47

RUDYARD KIPLING . . . . . . . 50

NATHANIEL &
   CHRISTOPHER LLOYD . . . 54

SIR GERALD LODER
   & FAMILY . . . . . . . . . . . . 58

SARAH RAVEN . . . . . . . . . . 62

WILLIAM ROBINSON . . . . . . .65

ARTHUR G. SOAMES . . . . . . . 71

SIR FREDERICK STERN . . . . . 73

ANGUS WHITE. . . . . . . . . . . .76

FRANCES WOLSELEY . . . . . . . 80

MORE INSPIRING
   SUSSEX GARDENERS . . . . . 86

INDEX . . . . . . . . . . . . . . . . . 94

# FOREWORD

Can you separate the gardener from their garden or the man from his masterpiece? I believe so, and more importantly the gardener is all too often more interesting than the garden! For that magic space is much more than just a collection of plants, though the mood which they create is important; the real creativity comes in designing the production itself, of which the plants are just a part. (Being a garden designer, I would say that, wouldn't I, though Walter Godfrey – designer, architect and antiquarian – had said it all before me.)

One would like to think that into a garden design its creator poured the cultural experience of his years, tempered by youthful memories, by travel and by his knowledge of location. I believe that Christopher Lloyd, for instance, did this; though in fact British gardeners generally tend towards an emphasis on the plantsman's skills alone, rather than innovative design. We remain a bit 'trad', for we are generally unreceptive to the influence of new ideas expressed in either fine arts or in other fields of design. It is interesting to discover the background to our gardeners and to find this view rather substantiated by remaining established gardens, although a younger generation is becoming more practical and is more concerned with food production and certainly with ongoing maintenance.

We have a dichotomy emerging in the gardening world that its writers and gardeners haven't really resolved yet, remaining rather in one camp or the other. It is the traditional classic ordered garden, which has frayed a bit at the edges and which we disguise by calling it wild and romantic, versus a newer, greener 20th-century aesthetic which becomes more concerned with location, fitness for place and sustainability.

Sir Frederick Stern was an early pioneer, for instance – he had to be, gardening in a Worthing chalk quarry. It could of course be argued that this greener way is just another fashion, like sunken gardens, Japanese or white ones, but this new mode seems more connected to a general philosophy and has yet to be properly worked through horticulturally. Are we still happy that the excellence of our gardens is merited by the number of alien plants we grow – tree ferns, eucalyptus, palms and the like – and if we are, what does this do to our Sussex landscapes? Does the formal style of garden sit well amongst free-form rolling downland or by the sea?

It comes down to horses for courses, and it is noticeable how many of our inspiring gardeners are also extremely sensitive to landscape as well. And there's the crunch: it is learning to look and ask oneself – given that you are lucky enough to have a view – 'do I want to see an alien shocker in the middle of it?' It can sometimes work, usually not! But if my space is tiny and urban, does it matter what I grow in it – and the answer is 'No it doesn't'.

But this new way runs far deeper than what we grow, and it is connected to sensitivity and a caring for Sussex itself. Cover it over with decking if you wish, but you are the loser. The rich understanding between people and their ground is not just about plants and scenery, it takes us deeper to where the land might reflect back to us its purpose and belonging. The land is so vulnerable and we are its caretakers, no matter how small our patch of it, for such a short time – it is the gardener, I believe, who for whatever reason – creative, therapeutic or economic – has felt this through his working of his own plot of land.

There is a spirituality in some of the writings of our authors who really feel this connection to our soil – as sticky or as chalky as it might be – and when they tap into this they are truly inspiring gardeners.

**JOHN BROOKES**

# INTRODUCTION

*'For dust thou art, and unto dust shalt thou return.'*

GENESIS CH. 3.V.19

This may seem rather a doom-laden quote to introduce what I sincerely hope will be an enjoyable read, yet it cuts to the very heart of what I feel gardening and growing things are really about. Every plant a gardener tends, be it the humblest tomato that is sown early in the year as a tiny white seed then grows, bears fruit and dies in the autumn, or the largest oak tree that completes its seasonal cycle year after year and will long outlive the person who planted it, demonstrates again and again this fundamental and inescapable principle of life.

Gardening is one of the most elemental and life-affirming activities we can undertake as it continually reasserts and reconnects us to nature. It is also productive, creative and simply makes one feel much better. Octavia Hill was one of the founder members of the National Trust and the organisation's first 'rescued' building was in Sussex, the Clergy House on the Tye in Alfriston. She wrote very convincingly of the importance of experiencing and connecting directly with nature: 'The need of quiet, the need of exercise, and the sight of sky and of things growing seem human needs common to all men.' Researching the people I feature in this book has illustrated just how universal the appeal of gardening is, as although there are common themes and characteristics that some gardeners share there are also quite as many differences, be they social, economic, cultural or aesthetic. Yet, however personally diverse my assembled group of gardeners is, they are all united by the desire, or indeed the need, to grow things.

How then did I make my selection? Well, certainly personally I do find each of my chosen subjects inspiring but often for differing reasons. During my research I found it interesting to discover just how many of these figures could be considered as something of renaissance men and women – they excel in several fields not just as gardeners (but then who is ever just one thing?). Another common theme that emerged was the rather maverick nature of many of these people; often they slip outside or sidestep their preordained roles in life. Particularly for women of the Edwardian era, such as Olive Cockerell, Helen Nussey and Frances Wolseley and her students, gardening was a way to evade the rigid social expectations of their time and class, a route to independence.

My choice of gardeners could not always be made using the obvious criterion of the gardens they created, as some no longer exist or are accessible. Gardens are living things and so especially vulnerable to change. The work of a painter, musician, writer or even an architect is far more permanent and by its nature less susceptible to damage, change or loss. Even where gardens have survived, and even blossomed under subsequent guardians, they would often not always be instantly recognisable were their original creators to time travel and visit them today. Even those gardens that aim to reflect a certain historical moment in their creators' lives, such as Charleston Farmhouse or Bateman's, can at best be only an approximation. Maybe it is more productive to think of a garden's spirit surviving rather than a more faithful facsimile.

So, if not the tangible legacy of their gardens, then what other things have attracted me to some of the gardeners featured here? As this is a book about Sussex gardeners, William Borrer's contribution to the collection and preservation of the county's native plants is of obvious importance. As already highlighted, I find the social history and gender issues surrounding Olive Cockerell, Helen Nussey and Frances Wolseley particularly fascinating. If Arthur Hellyer's living garden is no longer accessible then his prodigious written output certainly is.

Gardening encompasses many disciplines including science, history and architecture but for me a strong visual awareness must be evident in all successful and aesthetically pleasing gardens. While the painters Vanessa Bell and Derek Jarman and designer John Brookes are here, others who have no formal art training abound, yet their gardens are also visual feasts; look to those of Graham Gough, Christopher Lloyd, Sarah Raven and Angus White. For each the arrangement of colour, form and texture is obviously paramount. I think virtually all the gardeners featured in this book have cared passionately not just about how well their plants grew but also how well they looked arranged in their particular environments.

Naturally the history of gardens and gardening does not develop in isolation, detached from the broader social and economic trends of the day; it is as much a reflection of the social history of the times as other human endeavours. The rise and subsequent decline and fall of grand private gardens in Britain are reflected in the history of such gardens in Sussex just as much as elsewhere. Sheffield Park, Wakehurst Place, West Dean, Gravetye Manor, Highdown, Bateman's and Great Dixter were all built on the fortunes and vision of individual owners and, most importantly, with a great deal of affordable labour. Today many of these gardens can only survive, and indeed prosper, under the ownership of organisations like the National Trust and other charitable bodies. Due to changed times they are simply not sustainable as privately owned paradises anymore. The upside of this is that so many more of us can now enjoy their delights but it is sadly rare for new gardens to be created on such a scale.

The gardens made by the contemporary figures I deal with – such as Architectural Plants, Denmans, Marchants, Perch Hill and Prospect Cottage – are, with the exception of the latter, far larger than most people's plots but are tiny in comparison with the expansive canvases that the likes of the Loders, William Robinson or Arthur Soames had to play with. Yet I would argue that these modern creations are quite as exciting and original as the grand and great gardens of earlier eras and, most importantly, they all have a much more direct relationship with the gardens that most of us have. We find ideas and inspiration in these places and each can teach us new ways to look at our own outdoor spaces. Indeed in the gardens of John Brookes, Graham Gough, Sarah Raven and Angus White you can not only find inspiration but also take home the plants with which to create your very own Eden!

Without wishing to over-generalise, I think in part it is correct to say that the motivations behind some of my chosen gardeners have changed significantly with the generations. Scientific study, the need to collect, categorise and name plants, was a big part of what William Borrer, the Loder family and Sir Frederick Stern were concerned with, while today's gardeners are understandably far more preoccupied with the environmental impact of what they do and, perhaps less predictably, with growing food. Never before have the inhabitants of the county had such choice and abundance of relatively cheap food available to them. Yet provenance, quality and concerns such as 'food miles', rather than need, are now a real motivating force behind many gardeners' interest in growing at least some of their own food. Nowhere is this more evident than at Perch Hill and West Dean. It is interesting to speculate just how my selected early 21st-century gardeners will be viewed by future garden historians, what they will be remembered for and if their gardens survive them. I certainly hope others in times to come will recognise their inspiring qualities as I have.

In this introduction I have rehearsed just some of the reasons why I find my chosen Sussex gardeners such an inspiration but, as you read about each individual, their very particular drives and motivations will emerge. Yet, to return to my original point, what remains common to them all is the need to grow things, to be a part of that unending cycle of birth, life and death. 'A time to be born, and a time to die; a time to plant, and a time to pluck up that which is planted;' (*Ecclesiastes* ch. 3, v. 1). Surely whoever penned these words must have been a gardener!

# VANESSA BELL & LEONARD WOOLF
## *1879-1961 & 1880-1969*

Pick up any cultural guide to Sussex and it will not be long before the well-rehearsed accounts of the lives and loves of the Bloomsbury Group put in an appearance. However, even though both of the most visited Bloomsbury shrines in the county, Charleston Farmhouse and Monk's House, each have stunning gardens, I do not think either of their creators are particularly thought of as 'gardeners'. This is a shame as both Vanessa Bell and Leonard Woolf expended considerable portions of their prodigious creative and physical efforts on their lovely plots and achieved results well above the ordinary.

If wishing to categorise Vanessa Bell I would use the term 'artist-gardener'; someone who primarily gardens for visual satisfaction, rather than horticultural attainment. Such gardeners often start as ignorant amateurs but invariably gain a high level of expertise, even if in some cases this is somewhat selective or unorthodox. (Others I would include in this category are Vita Sackville-West, Lawrence Johnston and more recently Derek Jarman, *see p.47.*) Although over many years Vanessa developed her garden at the foot of the Downs into a vibrant and living extension of her painter's palette, her immediate preoccupation when confronted with the unpromising patch was to provide food for her burgeoning household.

Vanessa and her entourage (two children, lover, lover's friend, occasionally visiting husband) arrived at Charleston in 1916. Duncan

Grant (lover) and David Garnett (lover's friend) were both conscientious objectors and engaged locally as farm workers. Vanessa's sister, Virginia Woolf, found the house for rent and wrote: 'He [Leonard] says the garden could be made lovely – there are fruit trees, and vegetables, and a most charming walk under trees'.[1] This was perhaps something of a persuasive understatement as the walled garden immediately to the rear of the house was virtually a potato field dotted with a few aging apple trees. But hunger is hunger and, like most country dwellers in wartime, Charleston's new inhabitants set about creating a full larder. Amongst the vegetables, chickens, ducks, rabbits, a pig and beehives could all be found. It was quite a contrast for a woman reared in the rarefied atmosphere of London's Hyde Park Gate.

After the war the house continued to be rented as a rural retreat, only becoming the principal home of Vanessa and Grant in 1939. Cessation of hostilities led to a reappraisal of the plot and it gradually began to bear more resemblance to a garden than a smallholding. A particularly radical transition was the new formality of layout introduced in the walled garden. The artist and critic Roger Fry imposed a strict grid of paths and lawns over the potatoes, while a terrace paved with a mosaic floor of broken crockery provided a sheltered suntrap. Fry's strong axes were soon softened (and in parts almost obliterated) by Vanessa's exuberant planting. Sunken ponds were installed, along with a growing number of idiosyncratic sculptures and ornaments. Despite Vita Sackville-West's impression of life at Charleston as 'very plain living and high thinking'[2], a playfulness and jollity pervades the garden. Indeed it was the setting for numerous family theatricals over the years and every August fireworks showered their sparks over the large pond to mark the birthday of Vanessa's younger son, Quentin.

Whatever the input offered by friends, family and paid help over the years, it was Vanessa who primarily tended and nurtured the beautiful

**1.** *Woolf, Virginia, letter to Vanessa Bell,* The Letters of Virginia Woolf, Vol. 2, *edited by Nigel Nicolson and Joanna Trautmann, Hogarth Press, London, 1976, p.118.*
**2.** *Quoted in* Vita: The Life of Vita Sackville-West, *Victoria Glendinning, Penguin, London, 1984, p.150.*

Charleston garden. It is a motif that appears again and again in her paintings, either glimpsed through a window or open door, or taking centre stage in a composition – *The Walled Garden* (*c.*1916) and *View into the Garden* (1926) are just two of many examples. She took obvious delight in capturing in oils the transient vibrancy of the bold flowers she grew from seed.

The austerities of World War II saw vegetables once more appearing in the Charleston flower beds (they had been confined to the paddock beyond the walled garden during the inter-war years) but the spirit of the garden survived largely unscathed. Vanessa wrote in August 1945: 'This place is like the sleeping beauty's house, – the figs meet the arbutus in the Folly, fuchsias grown almost right across the doorstep.'[3] Sadly her death in 1961 heralded the decline of the garden although Grant lived on at the house for many years until his death in 1978. Two years later the Charleston Trust was formed to save the house and garden and open them to the public. Thankfully, the garden has been artfully restored (under the guidance of Sir Peter Shepheard) and now displays much of its 1950s' spirit.

I am sure most people more readily associate the lofty figures of Leonard and Virginia Woolf with the chilly heights of intellectual endeavour rather than with anything resembling a cosy domestic idyll. Certainly, life at the Woolf's Sussex retreat, Monk's House, was not all bucolic calm yet in many ways it was highly domestic. Virginia not only made bread but also indulged a passion for bottling fruit and making jam, while Leonard was an enthusiastic and accomplished grower of flowers, fruit and vegetables.

Leonard's future role as gardener was obviously apparent to his wife from the beginning. After their first inspection of Monk's House she wrote in her diary: 'He was pleased beyond his expectation. The truth is he has the making of a fanatical lover of that garden.'[4] Then shortly after buying the house in 1919, she noted his preference for it over their previous home, Asheham: 'Leonard infinitely prefers this, chiefly on

3. Bell, *Vanessa*, Selected Letters, *August 25th 1945*, p.498.
4. *Woolf, Virginia*, Diary of Virginia Woolf, Vol. 1, *Hogarth Press, London, 1977*, p.287.

account of the garden, which pours pears and plums and apples and vegetables upon us.'[5] They inherited a gardener, William Dedman, from the previous owners and he proceeded to teach his new employer much horticultural wisdom.

Monk's House was originally bought as a weekend and holiday home away from the bustle of London. However, by the late 1920s the couple were increasingly in residence. Then, as the Nazi bombs fell with growing frequency on London, the Woolfs decamped to the country for even longer periods. Tragically, it was from this house that Virginia set out on her last journey on March 28th 1941. She drowned in the nearby River Ouse. Leonard lived on in the house until his own death in 1969. Two large elm trees originally grew in the garden, named Leonard and Virginia, and her ashes were scattered below them. Both now are gone.

The front of this rather modest, if much extended, 18th-century cottage meets the quiet country lane on which it is situated, consequently the entire garden is to the rear. In 1928 the adjoining Pond Croft Field was acquired, both to extend the size of the plot and to prevent any building taking place there. Thus the garden seems very large indeed for such a relatively small house. During the war this field was used by villagers to grow vegetables for the war effort. Such was Leonard's expertise by this time that he had ensured the household was self-sufficient in fruit, vegetables and honey. Several productive hives stood against the low church walls at the bottom of the garden for many years.

Over the years the former agricultural outbuildings that originally littered the garden were demolished. Some of their foundations are still visible today in the semi-enclosed areas that add structure and form to the space and elevate this garden above that of the usual cottage style. To enable him to indulge his passion for exotic blooms, Leonard erected heated greenhouses, including the one that still runs the whole length of the house. As late as 1968 a visitor remembers this greenhouse as a riot of colour with daturas, gloriosas, gloxinias and lilies all in bloom

5. *Woolf, Virginia, letter to Saxon Sidney-Turner,* The Letters of Virginia Woolf, Vol. 2, *op. cit., p.389.*

amid the cacti. Leonard busied himself with Hogarth Press work during the mornings then would head for the garden after lunch. He was a founder member and president of the Rodmell and District Horticultural Society and often won prizes at their annual shows. The Royal Horticultural Society, the National Cactus and Succulent Society and the Sussex Beekeepers Association also counted him among their members.

Later in life Leonard was to enjoy a loving relationship with Trekkie Parsons and his garden often features in his correspondence to her. In July 1951 he wrote:

> *I went into the garden for a moment at 11 and the scent of honeysuckle – which is a sheet of bloom – was amazing. The little hypeastum which I got from South Africa is most beautiful, bright red with a white centre. One of the criniums has shot up its flowers. Two flowers opened on the prickly pear.*
> *All my news, you see, is of flowers.*[6]

Volumes have been written about Leonard Woolf as a publisher, writer and 'A List' member of the infamous Bloomsbury group but perhaps the last words on the man as a gardener should be those written by Virginia. Indeed they are the very last she was to write in her diary: 'L. is doing the rhododendrons…'[7]

~~~~~

**6.** *Woolf, Leonard, letter to Trekkie Parsons,* Letters of Leonard Woolf, *edited by Frederic Spotts, Bloomsbury, London, 1992, p.491.*
**7.** *Woolf,* Virginia, Diary of Virginia Woolf, Vol. 5, *Hogarth Press, London, 1984, p.359.*

**Top Places**
❯ *Charleston Farmhouse, near Firle, tel. 01323 811265, website: www.charleston.org.uk*
❯ *Monk's House, Rodmell, tel. 01372 870001, website: www.nationaltrust.org.uk*

# WILLIAM BORRER
## *1781-1862*

More than a fair share of my chosen 'Sussex' gardeners originally hailed from elsewhere. By contrast William Borrer was very much a true son of the county. Born in Henfield, his father was William Borrer of Hurstpierpoint, a county landowner and high sheriff of Sussex. Borrer junior was a botanical expert on British plants and gathered what was considered the first serious and comprehensive collection of Sussex flora. In many ways William typifies that particularly Victorian breed of wealthy, educated and dedicated enthusiasts whose tireless devotion to their chosen subject contributed so much to the canon of knowledge.

As a young man William worked for the family farming business and travelled widely across the county on horseback. These forays afforded him ample opportunity to study and collect local flora. However, his botanical horizons were not confined to Sussex alone. As his interest grew he met or corresponded with many of the leading botanists of the day, among them Joseph Banks, Dawson Turner and William Jackson Hooker. With the latter he visited Scotland and France, greatly extending what had hitherto been his largely self-taught methods of observation, collection and cataloguing.

William was not only a collector but also an enthusiastic and accomplished grower. At his Henfield home, Barrow Hill (now the site of Mill Drive and Cedar Way estate), he grew an astounding range of British and hardy exotic species, with figures of well in excess of six and a half thousand commonly quoted. Although technically an untrained amateur, William's painstaking work was characterised by a keenly scientific and empirical approach. For example, those groups of plants whose species varied only in the subtlest of ways William planted side by side, thus enabling him to minutely examine their variations and differences. Despite his vast collection at home, he continued to faithfully observe plants in their natural habitat. In 1844 he discovered the cut grass *Leersia oryzoides* growing in the wild; hitherto it had only been known as a cultivated species.

William took a keen interest in and grew many varieties of the genera Rosa, Salix and Rubus, although some of his most notable work was in the area of cryptogamic biology (the study of plants that have no true flowers such as ferns, mosses, algae and fungi). He was especially fascinated by lichens, describing no less than 26 new lichens in *Hooker's Supplement to English Botany*, an important work that ran to five volumes published between 1829 and 1866. His other published work included contributions to *British Flora* (1830) and *Lichenenographia Britannica* (1839). However, it was his first publication in 1805 that most concerned the botany of his home county. To Turner and Dillwyn's *Botanist's Guide* William contributed a comprehensive list, with notes and descriptions, of the many algae, ferns, flowering plants, fungi and lichens found in Sussex.

Highly regarded as an unfailingly reliable and meticulous source, William unfortunately never published a full and comprehensive guide to his county's flora. Had he done so he would doubtless now be better remembered and more widely known. However, recognition by his contemporaries included fellowships of the Linnean Society and the Royal Society. His wonderful herbarium of British plants, including numerous species from Sussex, was left to Kew Gardens after his death and was widely acknowledged as a superior and valuable resource for fellow botanists.

Beyond the world of plants, William took a philanthropic and active interest in the education not only of his own offspring (which reached the impressive count of three sons and five daughters) but also of less fortunate local children. In 1812 he founded the Henfield Society for Educating the Poor and built schools both for girls and for infants on his own land. Following in his father's footsteps, William's own son, also named William (*1814-98*), became a noted naturalist and taxidermist and donated his collection, *The Birds of Sussex*, to Brighton Museum.

## Herbariums

A herbarium is a systematically arranged collection of dried plants. Such compilations were often assembled by highly skilled and knowledgeable amateurs and have proved invaluable to students of botany and plant conservation. Borrer's herbarium was donated to the Royal Botanic Gardens at Kew where resides the splendidly entitled Keeper of the Herbarium. The Kew Herbarium dates back to 1852 when the Rev. William A. Bromfield bequeathed his own collection (containing specimens contributed by Borrer) along with his library. Other donations followed, including those made by George Bentham, and the Herbarium grew. In 1866, the year following his death, former Kew Director Sir William Hooker's herbarium, library and correspondence were purchased for £1,000, further swelling the collection. Today the Herbarium collection at Kew comprises over seven million pressed plants and is of national and international importance.

**Top Work & Place**
- Botanist's Guide, *1805 (contributor)*
- *Borrer's Herbarium, Royal Botanic Gardens, Kew*

# JOHN BROOKES
*born 1933*

Garden visitors in Sussex are lucky enough to have one of the very best contemporary British gardens set within their locale, Denmans Garden at Fontwell. This garden illustrates and exemplifies the work of John Brookes, one of the most innovative and influential of modern garden designers and writers. His work is renowned all over the world and he is as much in demand today as ever.

John's career began with a one-year course in horticulture at Durham County Agricultural School. From here he took a three-year apprenticeship at the Nottingham Parks Department and then went on to study landscape design at University College, London. As a young man he worked in the offices of Brenda Colvin and Sylvia Crowe (*see p.87*). Both women were highly influential figures – during their careers each held the position of President of the Institute of Landscape Architects (later the Landscape Institute) – and did much to establish and pioneer the profession of landscape design. John then joined the staff of the magazine *Architectural Design* to which he gradually began to contribute pieces. In the mid-1960s, he set up in practice in London, mostly designing private urban gardens. After a period running the Inchbald School of Garden Design and then living abroad, he took over the running of Denmans Garden in 1980 from Joyce Robinson and began to work the garden we see today. Resident in the picturesque Clock House set within the grounds of Denmans, John also ran his influential design school from here until the late 1990s. He was awarded an MBE in 2004 for his services to Garden Design and Horticulture, and the same year won an Award of Distinction from the American Association of Professional Landscape Designers.

When I met John, he explained how the principles of his design style are very much rooted in the period in which he started practising: 'Now it's termed minimal, then it was called Modernism.' For years gardening in Britain had been dominated by the need to achieve horticultural excellence, to breed the best rose or the best clematis, but people began to look at the wider picture and consider how plants could be used within a well-designed and more considered context. The modern town dweller was receptive to new ways of looking at, and indeed of using, their precious garden spaces. Change was in the air.

In the early 1970s Terence Conran's *House Book* (to which John was a contributor) found an eager audience, keen to transform their houses in a stylish way, inside and out. Similarly John's earlier book *The Room Outside* (1969), had also struck a timely note. This book, like all John's work, is about designing spaces for people, to enhance and expand the way they live. He explains that he likes 'fishing about' clients, assessing their personality, tastes, interests and the ways in which they live. In this sense his philosophy is little changed. In 2006 he wrote: 'It's all very exciting as interest in design outside breaks away from interest in horticulture... people are still the common denominator when designing a garden – the space they need and how they move about in it.'[1] Hitherto the concept of the 'garden room' had been more associated with grand and expansive gardens like Sackville-West's Sissinghurst or Johnston's Hidcote. John showed those of us working on a more domestic scale how to make our gardens attractive and practical extensions to the home, quite literally 'rooms outside'.

Over the years John has also produced many successful books on garden design. However, these are not just packed with enticing and inspiring pictures of fabulous gardens (although certainly these are here

---

1. Brookes, John, Small Garden, *2006, Dorling Kindersley, London, p.6.*

in abundance) but primarily with substantial and practical information. He carefully analyses for the reader why, and most importantly how, a particular design works. The garden is always considered in relation to its environment, be that primarily architectural or situated in a more rural setting.

Many may most readily associate John Brookes with the modern garden placed within an urban environment, yet some of his most interesting work, and views, concern gardening in the country. He has designed over 230 gardens in Sussex alone. In his introduction to *The Country Garden* (1987) he states:

> Country living is more than logs and lambs, it is a way of life conditioned by the all-pervading surroundings, and in most countries those surroundings change very quickly from area to area, depending on the geology and traditional methods of farming. Country-livers must be prepared to become part of the scene and strengthen it, or our countryside will be lost.[2]

Not surprisingly, John's work is in demand all over the world and working abroad so much has given him the chance to study many varied landscapes and habitats. He loves to observe how plants associate naturally in the wild, and he feels their selective spacing and grouping have much to teach us. Such detailed study continually renews his work and he steadily veers away from transient trends. For instance, in the meadowland of the more temperate climate of Britain woody plants thrive, so why limit one's palette to the perennials and grasses so favoured by the fashionable prairie planters? For him planting in 'a wild way' means a sensitive consideration of the local habitat and climate.

John's writing is always refreshing, stimulating and expansive in a way that is rarely found in most modern garden books. In his 1994 book *Planting the Country Way* he dealt not just with gardens but also with geology, social history and ecology. As he explained, 'the conservationist's concern for the wild has got to me; I want to see the advent of spring through nature's eyes – the country way. I feel there has to be a

---

2. Brookes, John, The Country Garden, *Dorling Kindersley, London, 1987, p.6.*

coming together of tamed with wild.'[3] When taking an overview, there appears to be a smooth trajectory from John's early career to the present day, one that began with the radical modernist transformation of the typical small urban garden through to the later merging of the garden boundary with the countryside beyond. As he succinctly puts it, 'I began from the house looking out and now I'm in the countryside looking back towards the house.'

## Hons & gongs

As John Brookes MBE proves, the rewards of the gardening life are not always confined solely to the satisfaction achieved from surveying a newly dug bed or savouring the fragrance of a freshly picked bunch of flowers, occasionally recognition rains down from on high. Queen Victoria (1819-1901) was on the throne of Great Britain and Ireland for an astounding 63 years, making her the longest reigning monarch in British history. The eponymous Victoria Medal of Honour in Horticulture is conferred by the Royal Horticultural Society (RHS) and is regarded by British gardeners as one of the highest achievements in their field. The medal was established by the RHS in 1897 'in perpetual remembrance of Her Majesty's glorious reign, and to enable the Council to confer honour on British horticulturalists'. In recognition of Victoria's enduring reign, the number of recipients who can hold the medal at any one time is restricted to 63. Needless to say there are several deserving medal holders among the inspiring gardeners of Sussex including J.R.B. Evison, Gerald Loder (Lord Wakehurst), Sir Giles Loder, Arthur Hellyer and Christopher Lloyd. The latter two were also awarded the MBE and the OBE respectively. Another gardening Member of the British Empire is Nathaniel Lloyd, while, perhaps most impressively, Sir Frederick Stern of Highdown was awarded his knighthood for Services to Horticulture in 1956.

---

3. *Brookes, John,* Planting the Country Way, *BBC Books, London, 1994, p.10.*

**Top Works & Place**

❯ The Room Outside, *1969*

❯ The New Small Garden Book, *1991*

❯ *Denmans Garden, Fontwell, tel. 01243 542808, website: www.denmans-garden.co.uk*

# JIM BUCKLAND & SARAH WAIN
## *born 1954 & 1956*

My next inspiring Sussex gardeners are responsible for putting the lovely West Dean Gardens firmly on the map for any garden visitor to the county. Run by married couple Jim Buckland and Sarah Wain, the garden's unique selling point is the expertly restored and reinvigorated Victorian Walled Garden. However, this should in no way distract from the beautiful and varied areas that the other 90 or so acres have to offer.

Originally from London, Jim is an honours graduate from the Royal Botanic Gardens at Kew and it was there that he met his future wife. Sarah already had a Diploma in Horticultural Science from Burnley Horticultural College in her home town of Melbourne. Once in England she found her native expertise with exotics was in demand at Kew, where she spent three years in the Temperate Department. Following their time at Kew, Jim and Sarah spent over four years in Australia working in a variety of jobs, including local authority parks and tending the gardens at Parliament House in Melbourne. On returning to England they worked on a private estate, Lockerley Hall in Hampshire, where they redeveloped a much neglected garden, including a period walled garden.

In part it was the experience and interest in walled gardens that Jim and Sarah had developed at Lockerley that prompted their move to West Dean in 1991. At that time the grounds of the West Sussex estate were tired and lacked focus. Owned and run by a charitable trust, The

Edward James Foundation, the grand house that is the centrepiece of the estate is home to West Dean College, a renowned centre of excellence which teaches short courses in the arts, music and traditional crafts. At the time, much of the parkland was struggling to recover from the ravages of the 1987 storm, and the once fine walled fruit and kitchen gardens, with their extensive collection of glasshouses, were semi-derelict. Fortunately, there was the will and momentum from the trustees to invest in the restoration and development of the gardens, so for Jim it seemed 'the perfect job'. In addition, Sarah's expertise with hot houses made her an ideal candidate for the new venture, so she followed Jim to Sussex a few months later. And, as she points out, 'the beautiful setting on the South Downs and the generous average rainfall are all things I value highly as an Australian.'

Jim explained to me his plan once at West Dean: 'Initially it was to formulate a vision of where we should go, to set objectives and goals. Most importantly, we needed to work out how to achieve these and then sustain them. It is the ongoing management and development of a garden that is often neglected in the excitement to make or restore a place.' It should be remembered that back in the early 1990s walled kitchen gardens were considered something of an anachronism. In its Edwardian heyday, the productive West Dean kitchen garden had employed half the garden workforce of the whole grounds (11 men out of a total of 22). By the 1920s, the demise of available and affordable garden labour, coupled with cheaper and more plentiful imports of food, heralded the decline of large-scale private fruit and vegetable gardens. Inevitably, with the gardens went much of the skill and knowledge to maintain and manage them.

In 1987 the BBC broadcast a series of television programmes called *The Victorian Kitchen Garden*. Presented by the late Harry Dodson (who had worked at Ashburnham Place in Sussex before World War II) and Peter Thoday, the programmes followed the restoration and working of a productive walled garden. The series was a firm favourite with Jim and Sarah and did much to raise the general awareness of the sad plight of many such gardens. Then, just as Jim and Sarah were settling into West

Dean, the restoration of the large vegetable gardens at Heligan in Cornwall was commencing. Thus they found themselves in the vanguard of a resurgence of interest in traditional methods of growing food. Since that time, concerns about sourcing locally grown produce, the popularity of farmers' markets and an increased interest in self-sufficiency have all contributed to vegetables and fruit being considered sexy in a way that was unimaginable when Jim and Sarah first started on their own mission to 'recapture the flavour of the turn-of-the-century garden'!

One of the huge successes of Jim and Sarah's time at West Dean has been their increasingly popular events. These include the Wholly Herb Show in spring, followed by the Garden and Art Event, the Chilli Fiesta, the Totally Tomato Show and then the autumn Apple Affair. The idea for the chilli event was prompted by a visit to New York where Jim and Sarah noted that the Brooklyn Botanical Garden was hosting a Chilli Festival. They already had a few chillies growing back home in the greenhouses, originally raised at the request of one of the college tutors who needed interesting plants for a botanical illustration class. Fired with enthusiasm, Jim and Sarah started with a small event. They now grow over 250 different varieties of chilli and 110 stallholders attend the event annually, visitors flocking in their droves. West Dean-grown produce is similarly well represented at the Totally Tomato Show as they grow something approaching 200 types. This all adds to the diversity of life at West Dean, as Sarah notes: 'I love the variety of work, the daily challenges and the continual learning process required to maintain and lift standards of horticulture here.'

Such has been the success of the Walled Garden restoration and the annual shows that people sometimes overlook the other areas of parkland and garden at West Dean. Of prime importance is the wonderful St Roche's Arboretum, which for Jim is 'the icing on the cake'. It dates back to the 1830s and 1840s and is home to a variety of native and exotic trees. A long-term programme of planting and refining is well under way and this expansive area has a subtlety and calm that more than rewards those visitors who venture away from the attractions closer to the main house. The Arboretum also boasts pockets of ericaceous soil (in contrast to the mainly chalky conditions elsewhere) so rhododendrons flourish here, another example of the huge variety to be found at West Dean. Like Sarah, it is this variety that Jim loves: 'Here we cover practically every area of horticulture – fruit, vegetables, a wide range of plants grown under glass, the pergola, along with the spring garden and wild garden.'

Jim and Sarah do not only work as a good partnership but more importantly operate as part of a committed team. There are ten full-time gardeners at West Dean plus one seasonal worker and between 20 to 30 volunteers. For Sarah this is a particularly satisfying part of her work: 'I love passing on information to either trainees or the volunteers. I try and teach the basic craft of horticulture to give confidence and expertise to them, so they can get the same kick out of the work that I do.' The ordered state of Jim's Gardens Manager's office is testimony to the organised running of the team throughout the seasons. Jim's other strengths are his knowledge of hard landscaping, both theoretical and practical, and trees and shrubs. Alongside being a 'glasshouse person', Sarah is an accomplished grower and plantswoman who also has a keen eye for colour. She is the first woman to have been invited to join the Vegetable Trials Sub-Committee, a prestigious RHS post. The pleasure and satisfaction they gain from their work is obvious. To quote Sarah: 'It is a real privilege to do a job you love doing; it brings a real freedom with it, is creative and gives pleasure to others.'

Although most of the major plans for the garden have now been achieved, the pair consider there is still much to do in the future. One of their concerns from the outset has been to ensure that the ongoing sustainability of the gardens is managed properly. As plants and plans mature, subtle adjustments must be made continually if the grounds are to develop and progress. No garden is static and the best are those that respond sensitively to inevitable changes. As Jim puts it: 'There is a continuity to gardening; it is cyclical but it is not the same.'

**Top Place**

⯈ *West Dean Gardens, West Dean, tel. 01243 811301, website: www.westdean.org.uk*

# OLIVE J. COCKERELL & HELEN NUSSEY
## *born 1869 & 1875-1965*

Olive Cockerell and Helen Nussey certainly qualify for the prize for being the most obscure gardeners in this book. I first encountered them while browsing the shelves of the Lindley Library in London where I found the delightful little book *A French Garden in England: A Record of the Successes and Failures of a First Year of Intensive Culture*. Published in 1909, it was written by Helen and illustrated by Olive. If obscure, it is also extremely inspiring, as it chronicles the valiant attempt of two young Edwardian women to lead useful, independent and 'free' lives.

First let me disabuse readers of any misleading notions of elegant parterres or chic finishing schools suggested by the terms 'French garden' and 'intensive culture'. We are talking hot beds here, the heat generated by manure, and lots of it, not Gallic passions! French Gardening was a long-established intensive method of growing large quantities of crops in a comparatively small area using manure-filled frames, glazed lights and bell-glasses. The use of the system was largely curtailed by the growth of motorised transport and the consequent demise of the horse, as the women explain: 'Fresh straw manure from the stables of well-fed horses is what is required'.[1] Using these cultivation methods, Helen and Olive set about establishing their own market garden.

---

1. *Nussey, Helen and Cockerell, O.J.*, A French Garden in England: A Record of the Successes and Failures of a First Year of Intensive Culture, *Stead's Publishing House, London, 1909, p.69.*

Both women had been pupils at a well-established market garden but had no experience of running their own concern. However, they were 'eager to live health-giving lives in the country after some years of town life, and it was necessary for us to be earning in the near future'.[2]

Certainly they were aware that they were part of the one million 'surplus women' identified in the 1901 census and, like Frances Wolseley's students (*see p. 80*), would have to make their own way in the world. After exhaustive cycling trips in search of suitable premises, they were finally offered a lease on a lodge and two acres (0.8 hectares) of land on a friend's Sussex estate. Although never identified in the book, contemporary commercial directories list it as 'The Bungalow', Shipley, just south of Horsham. Here they could 'see miles of wooded country and the blue line of the South Downs swelling up to Chanctonbury Ring in the distance clear before us.'[3] They go on to paint a seductively enticing scene: 'we ourselves, a little way from the village, were quite hidden in the woods, entirely to our liking, for the life we were going to lead was to be free, as near the life of the woods as we could make it.'[4]

The establishment of the market garden was hard, challenging work, and so physically demanding that they vowed to make their domestic duties as light and simple as possible, so they could devote the maximum energy to the task in hand. They lived mainly on nuts and cheese, eschewing the local butcher: 'We could not have joints of raw meat desecrating such a sanctum.'[5] Aided by outside help, work on their 'raw field' began in January 1908 and their first summer was one of experimentation. With this system of production, soil preparation is everything. After the initial digging of the site by outside help, all subsequent cultivation was done by Helen and Olive, aided by a boy and the donkey, Johnnie. As the garden developed they took pupils, thus swelling the workforce. 'We never thought of the time, we just worked till dark; and when the moon shone we worked under the stars.'[6] By the end of their inaugural year they had achieved much; excellent soil, healthy

2. Nussey, Helen and Cockerell, O.J., A French Garden in England: A Record of the Successes and Failures of a First Year of Intensive Culture, Stead's Publishing House, London, 1909, p.8.
3. Ibid., p.13.  4. Ibid., p.14.  5. Ibid., p.14.  6. Ibid., p.21.

produce, eager customers and paying pupils. The crops they grew included melons, cauliflowers, strawberries, French beans, tomatoes, lettuces, carrots, turnips, cucumbers and asparagus, along with some soft fruit and roses. All were popular with private customers who valued the taste and freshness of their produce. But beyond the commercial success lay a deeper satisfaction, one I think best expressed in their own words.

> Health, bright skies, congenial companionship, the visits of our friends, the sympathy and help of all around, the knowledge that we were making steady progress in what we had set ourselves to do; the many creature comrades who lived with us in the wood; the freshness of the dawn; the awakening of the birds; the smell of the mossy earth; the pushing of the growing things in the spring; the moon behind the trees – the colour of it all! And then the long winter evenings with a log fire and a pleasant book and the consciousness of a good day's work done. Surely there is little else that heart of human can desire.[7]

The lyricism of the prose is equally matched by Olive's lovely black and white line drawings scattered through the text. Alongside the Beatrix Potter-like charm of rabbits nibbling lettuces and mice enjoying the cauliflowers, sit clear and skilful drawings of their water pump and the technicalities of frame construction. However it is the drawing entitled *Aches and Pains*, showing one of the women stretching to the heavens, spade laid aside a moment mid-digging, that surely speaks most eloquently to any gardener.

What then became of our gardening pioneers? Their commercial listing as market gardeners ceases after 1911 and sadly there is scant biographical information on Olive. She puts in an appearance in the 1901 census as having been born in Dulwich, London, in 1869 and is described as a 'black and white artist'. Information on Helen Georgiana Nussey is far more forthcoming. Born in Richmond, London, she was educated at Cheltenham Ladies College and, prior to her French

---

7. Nussey, Helen and Cockerell, O.J., A French Garden in England: A Record of the Successes and Failures of a First Year of Intensive Culture, *Stead's Publishing House, London, 1909, p.154.*

Gardening days, was the first almoner at London's Westminster Hospital. Certainly by 1914 she must have ceased gardening professionally as she was employed as one of two principal assistant organisers for the London County Council's school care service. Until her retirement in 1940, she was involved in working with the capital's poor children in various capacities, including the establishment of spectacle clubs (to raise funds for glasses for poor-sighted pupils) and organising evacuees during World War II. For her social work she was awarded an OBE. Helen's horticultural interests continued through her involvement with the London Gardens Society and she published two further books, *London Gardens of the Past* (1938) and *Miniature Alpine Gardens* (1949). Do track down a copy of *A French Garden in England* if you can, then curl up for a couple of happy hours with this inspiring little read.

## An apple a day

Olive and Helen's market garden was sadly too short-lived to establish an orchard, but many others flourished across the county. Kent has long been referred to as 'the garden of England' but anyone who has visited some of the wonderful gardens of Sussex will doubtless feel the title really belongs to its neighbouring county. Much of Kent's claim to this sobriquet rests on its traditional growing of fruit, especially apples, however Sussex has also been known to produce a mean apple or two.

In the 1870s Lord Egremont of Petworth raised the eponymous 'Egremont Russet'. While undoubtedly delicious, one wonders if its great commercial success is in part attributable to its aristocratic name, which rather overshadows that other Sussex strain, the less grandly titled 'Knobbly Russet' (raised earlier in the century at Midhurst). A brief list of some old Sussex varieties is evidence enough of just how widely spread apple growing has been across the county – 'Ashdown Seedling', 'Crawley Beauty', 'Eastbourne Pippin', 'Goodwood Pippin' and 'Wadhurst Pippin' are just a few.

Rather confusingly, the cooking apple 'Alfriston' was raised at Uckfield in the late 18th century by a Mr Shepherd. Known then as 'Shepherd's Seedling' or 'Shepherd's Pippin', it was renamed in 1819 by Alfriston resident Mr Brookes. In the same year it won an RHS Award of Merit. Described enticingly as 'large, sugary and brisk', its sweet, pear-like flavour was much in demand but is rarely tasted today. From the mid-19th century we have 'Forge', a popular apple useful for cooking and eating. It hails from the industrial iron areas around East Grinstead and Crawley, hence its name. 'Forge' was one of the apple varieties grown by William Robinson (see p.65) at Gravetye Manor.

As might be expected, there are some wonderful stories attached to many of these varieties (whether apocryphal or not is hard say). In the 1770s, Uckfield blacksmith Mr Turley is said to have tossed a quantity of cider pomace (the pulp left after apple pressing) over his garden hedge. From this unpromising medium magnificently rose the apple 'Mannington's Pearmain'. Turley's grandson, John Mannington, sent the family strain to the RHS in 1847. From little acorns…

Given their resources and horticultural expertise, it is perhaps not surprising that several varieties of Sussex apples were developed on the county's estates. Petworth has already been mentioned and head gardener Fred Streeter raised 'Duck's Bill' there in 1937. H.C. Princep at Buxted Park produced 'Coronation' while Parham Park's 'Golden Pippin' is a small, sweet 17th-century variety. Sidney Ford, head gardener at Leonardslee, raised 'Doctor Hogg' in 1880, christened after the Victorian pomologist Robert Hogg. It won the First Class Certificate from the RHS in 1878.

Though not widely available at supermarkets and greengrocers, some of these varieties can be purchased in autumn at the Middle Farm Shop in Firle, which is also home to the National Collection of Cider and Perry. Both Middle Farm and West Dean Gardens (see p.24) hold annual Apple Days where a wide range of varieties can be sampled. And of course, if you have the space, you can always plant your own mini Sussex orchard, thus helping to keep these old varieties alive and well. Other Sussex delicacies include the pea, 'Simpson's Special', from Mr Simpson of Petworth and the tomato 'Darby Striped'. Dr Lewis Darby was research fellow at the Glasshouse Crops Research Institute in Littlehampton in the 1960s when he developed the strain, which sound beautiful, being variously striped red and green, red and yellow, pink and yellow or yellow and green.

**Cockerell's Top Work**
❯ A French Garden in England, *1909*

**Nussey's Top Works**
❯ A French Garden in England, *1909*
❯ London Gardens of the Past, *1938*
❯ Miniature Alpine Gardens, *1949*

# J.R.B. EVISON
## 1909-81

The life-enhancing nature of our public parks and gardens is something that should be recognised by everyone and their preservation and maintenance dearly fought for. In particular, residents and visitors to Brighton should say a silent 'thank you' to Ray Evison every time they take a stroll in one of its fine parks. As his obituary states:

> ... he was undoubtedly the most eminent Parks superintendent of his generation. The parks and open spaces at Brighton rival its architecture in beauty and reputation ... They are his tangible memorial; his insistence on high standards of cultivation and maintenance ensures that they will long remain as witness of Brighton's debt to him.[1]

John Raymond Berridge Evison (most often referred to as 'Ray') moved from Manchester in 1930 to work as a journeyman gardener at the Royal Horticultural Society's gardens at Wisley in Surrey. Two years later he transferred from being an employee to become a student gardener. Ray quickly excelled himself and passed a series of examinations, including the National Diploma in Horticulture. Armed with an array of qualifications, he arrived in Sussex towards the end of 1933 to take up the position of Superintendent of the Floral Department at Brighton Parks. By 1935 he

---

1. Aberconway, 'John Raymond Berridge Evison OBE, NDH', Garden, 1981, p.295.

was Assistant Superintendent of the whole department, then Deputy Superintendent and finally Director of Brighton's Parks and Gardens. In all he gave 40 years' service to the town and received an OBE in 1970.

During World War II, just as elsewhere, much of Brighton's public parks and gardens land was exploited as part of the war effort to produce home-grown food. Expert gardeners were vital to this effort and Ray worked alongside the well-known horticulturalists G.C. Johnson and R.T. Pearl on the East Sussex War Agricultural Executive Committee. Not only were public spaces turned from floral displays to cabbage patches but the committee was also instrumental in encouraging and advising the public on growing their own produce.

After the war, Ray's considerable talents and energies were directed once again to making the town's parks, gardens and open spaces oases of beauty and calm. Preston Park was always one of his favourites and from his earliest days in the department he took a particular interest in its splendid Rock Garden. The park's exuberant and colourful 'Gardens of Greeting', which run alongside the main London Road to the east, still delight visitors driving into the town today and were another of Ray's special interests. In 1953 he designed the Garden for the Blind, a gift to the people of the town from both Brighton Corporation and the Butchers of Brighton, Hove and Portslade, to commemorate the coronation of Elizabeth II.

Sussex of course is a coastal county which presents particular challenges for those who garden at its southerly extremes. As one experienced in tending the windswept parks of Brighton, Ray had some informed and illuminating observations on the subject and wrote an interesting article on seaside gardens. The standard of his garden writing rises well above that of the merely instructive and always makes for an enjoyable read. He begins in a typically engaging and evocative way: 'It is November as I write, the wind has been rising for some hours and half-a-mile away high seas are running. Greenhouse ventilators have long been closed and frames not only closed but battened down.'[2] He goes on to say that

2. Evison, J.R.B., 'A Garden by the Sea', Journal of the RHS, Vol. LXXIX, Part 6, June 1954, p.294.

those who do not live by the sea tend to picture seaside gardens bathed in summer sunshine but warns:

> *Just as holidays are fleeting, so are perfect days, and winds too are by no means a prerogative of winter. A few years ago I recall the replanting of a chain of gardens right upon the sea-front no fewer than seven times between early June and late July. Equinoxial gales are certainly no mariners' myth!*[3]

Always an enthusiastic communicator and educator, he conveys much practical advice on creating a successful and resilient coastal garden but always interspersed with lyrical passages; for example, of Spanish gorse (*Genista hispanica*) he writes: 'It will then roll out into a veritable miniature South Downs of deep green spring branchlets.'[4]

Ray was a very active and supportive member of the RHS, serving on the Wisley Advisory Committee, was chairman of both the Joint Chrysanthemum Committee and the Examination Board and then became Vice President of the Society. In 1968 he was awarded their highest accolade, the Victoria Medal of Honour. Another distinguished post he held was that of President of the Institute of Park and Recreation Administration in 1966-7. Yet despite such high honours and achievements, his living legacy still remains the lovely open spaces of Brighton, so do please remember him when you are next there.

---

**3.** Evison, J. R. B., 'A Garden by the Sea', Journal of the RHS, *Vol. LXXIX, Part 6, June 1954, p.294.*
**4.** Ibid., *p.302.*

**Top Works**
- Gardening for Display, *1958*
- Saturday in My Garden, *1961*

# WALTER H. GODFREY
## *1881 - 1961*

Today Walter Hindes Godfrey is remembered mostly as an architect and antiquarian rather than as a landscape or garden designer. Indeed it was his desire to ensure that the buildings he worked on were situated within an appropriate setting that was his main concern and interest, rather than matters horticultural. Yet he restored and conserved a large number of Sussex houses of varying importance and in the process undoubtedly contributed to the richness and quality of the county's gardens.

Born in Hackney, London, Walter trained as an architect at the Central School of Arts and Crafts. He was articled to James Williams who was continuing the busy country house practice of George Devey following his death. Walter Godfrey then went on to work for the London County Council where his enthusiastic interest in antiquities led to his involvement with the Committee for the Survey of London. He edited several monographs based on the survey. In 1903 Walter returned to his previous practice, now run by Edmund Wratten. Walter and Wratten set up in partnership in 1905. This relationship was further cemented when Walter married Wratten's sister Gertrude in 1907. Apart from a spell in the Ministry of Munitions during World War I, the two continued in partnership until Wratten's death in 1925. The following year Walter became a fellow of the Royal Institute of British Architects. In the early 1940s he was appointed director of the newly formed National

Buildings Record (now the National Monuments Record) created to record historic buildings.

Walter's long association with Sussex began in 1905 with the extension of one of the county's many bungalows, a modest start but one to be superseded in time by various manors and even a castle! He and his family (he had four children) leased a cottage, 'Corners', in Buxted. The death of his partner, followed by the Depression of the 1930s, brought to an end Walter's London practice. In 1932 he moved to Lewes and opened up offices at 203, High Street. This proved a good move as he was promptly asked by Sir Paul Latham to complete the restoration of Herstmonceux Castle, his most high profile commission. On completion, architectural historian Christopher Hussey wrote: 'With his learning, artistic sense, and first rate practical ability, Mr. Godfrey has been an ideal architect for handling so precious a possession as the Castle.'[1] He went on: 'The garden now, though following the same lines as before, has a new, a contemporary, cleanliness and spaciousness.'[2]

Another notable commission in the county was the work Walter undertook on the house and gardens at Charleston Manor, Litlington. In 1931 the society portrait painter Sir Oswald Birley and his wife Rhoda purchased the manor and employed Walter to restore the house and lay out the grounds. The manor, along with its magnificent tithe barn, was set picturesquely, if rather inconveniently, amid a farmyard. Walter's layout out for the garden rested on the traditional premise of self-contained areas or compartments. The garden does not embrace vistas of the surrounding landscape, rather it is inward-looking, sheltered by the surrounding edges of Friston Forest. Shelter and privacy were some of the guiding principles in Walter's garden design work and occur frequently in his writing. Other signature devices used here are circular steps, generous terraces and pathways, along with yew, box, holly and beech hedges. The strict architectural bones of his design were softened by the planting of Lady Birley, a passionate gardener.

---

1. Hussey, Christopher, 'The Restoration of Hermonceux Castle', Country Life, November 30th 1953, p.568.
2. Ibid., p.572.

Long before the move to Sussex, Walter had become involved with designing the surrounding grounds in which his buildings were set. Like many architects he was unhappy to leave the arrangement of these spaces to others, especially if they were horticulturalists. As would be expected in the 'Battle of the Styles', he was very much on the side of Reginald Blomfield, as opposed to William Robinson (*see p.65*). In 1914, he published *Gardens in the Making*. To the modern audience his prose may seem somewhat stilted but the reader is left in no doubt as to the primary importance of the implementation of design rules when laying out a garden. He writes: 'Horticulture is, indeed, a proud science, but its votaries surely assume too much when they state that a knowledge of plants and shrubs is synonymous with the power of design.'[3] A little later he continues: 'The untrained eye – and the age is full of untrained eyes where art is concerned – admires the effect of a skilfully planted garden, but is seldom capable of seeing that there are serious principles involved, or that without them such effects would be impossible.'[4]

Walter's garden design work more or less ceased after World War II. He could never be classed as a radical or influential designer (nor does one get the impression that he would have wished to be) yet his work is characterised by a restraint and formal simplicity that seem to sit most comfortably with old English houses. Always built to the best possible quality, his architectural work was based on sound and solid knowledge. He spent much of his life engaged on painstakingly detailed surveying, recording and restoration, thus ensuring that many middle-ranking, and a few major, Sussex houses were restored with an unusual level of care and consideration. Sadly this quiet and erudite antiquarian now seems very much of another age.

---

**3.** *Godfrey, Walter H.,* Gardens in the Making, *B.T. Batsford, London, 1914, p.1.*
**4.** *Ibid., p.3.*

**Top Places & Work**
- ◐ *Herstmonceux Castle, tel. 01323 833816, website: www.herstmonceux-castle.com*
- ◐ *Charleston Manor, Litlington, website: www.charleston-manor.org.uk*
- ◐ *Elm Tree Farm, West Wittering*
- ◐ *Gardens in the Making, 1914*

# GRAHAM GOUGH

*born 1956*

Although I find all my Sussex subjects inspiring, I feel that the adjective is at its most fitting when applied to Graham Gough and the wonderful garden and nursery he has created from so little. The success of the Marchants garden and its complete fittingness to place, is the direct result of Graham's background. Born and bred in the county, the South Downs were his playground and as a young man the place he always came back to. He belongs here, and the garden he has created most certainly feels it belongs here, too.

Graham was born and grew up on the coast, at Newhaven. His musical talents and fine singing voice were recognised early and he studied at the Guildhall School of Music in London, successfully turning professional in 1981. But as Graham explains, 'I'm not a townie and used to come back to my parents' home at Newhaven most weekends.' On these visits he noticed that the next-door neighbours could no longer tend their vegetable patch and offered to work it for them. Soon he was racing back to Sussex every Friday night, so eager to get out in the garden that he would dig in the dark! 'That vegetable garden became an obsession and a therapeutic break from the demands of London.' Graham decided to take a year's sabbatical, move back to Sussex and review his future.

Graham began to work as a jobbing gardener. Among his customers was the great plantswoman and eccentric Katie Pickard-Smith at Glynde (it was not unheard of for Graham to enter her cottage and be confronted with an iguana sitting on top of the television). She taught Graham a great amount about plants and he still cites her as an important influence. At the same time, he was augmenting his admittedly scanty horticultural education by frequent visits to the gardens at Great Dixter (*see p.54*) and Sissinghurst. The latter Graham considers to have been 'fundamental to me, and it had the great advantage of every plant being accurately labelled'. He soon knew the name and position of virtually every plant in the garden. It was on one of his Sissinghurst visits that he spotted a specimen of the then rare chocolate-coloured *Cosmos astrosanguineus*. On enquiring where he might obtain it, head gardeners Sibylle Kreutsberger and Pam Schwerdt sent him off to the nearby Washfield Nursery at Hawkhurst. This was a real plantsman's paradise, run by the highly knowledgeable Elizabeth Strangman. Not surprisingly, Graham soon became a regular customer at Washfield, buying plants for the various downland gardens he was tending. He then began full-time employment at the nursery, learning everything he could about plants and propagation, 'almost by osmosis', as he puts it, finally ending up as a partner in the business. Plants have remained fundamental to what Graham does: 'I've always been driven by an interest in plants, along with design and cultivation. I love the craft of growing plants; vegetable growing is very much a craft. Plants are the tools for making a beautiful garden. I treat them as an artist might treat colours.' At Marchants he propagates on site almost everything he sells at the nursery.

In 1998 Graham and his wife, the textile designer Lucy Goffin, were scouring the Sussex countryside looking for a place to live and create a nursery and garden. They very much wanted a blank canvas and that's certainly what they found at 2 Marchants Cottages, Laughton. The small Victorian cottage came with two acres (0.8 hectares) of uneven ground, dotted with broken drains, abandoned cars and armies of competing weeds. It was also south-facing with the most stupendous views framed by the Downs. And so they set about making the beautiful and innovative garden, rich in colour, texture and movement, that today is Marchants Hardy Plants.

Surprisingly, Graham felt undaunted by the task ahead. With Lucy beside him and happily ensconced in their new home, he felt a creative freedom: 'At last I could use my accumulated plant knowledge and I found this a very inspiring place to be.' However, the soil proved to be far less fertile and workable than Graham had first believed. Thus he set about the mammoth task of adding tons upon tons of coarse grit, home-made compost, finished with a top-dressing of mushroom compost, wheelbarrow full by wheelbarrow full. Few gardeners I think can boast (or bemoan) quite such an intimate relationship with their soil. Certainly, the ground at Marchants has left Graham feeling compromised and frustrated at times. 'Here the soil is mean and tight, and bloody hard work! We give so much to a garden and hope it gives us something back, but sometimes this garden has felt slow to give returns.' The upside is that the enforced limited palette of having to grow only those plants that thrive in these particular conditions has resulted in a garden that is in total harmony with its setting, nothing jars or is forced, everything looks at home here (including Graham).

Having given so much to his new life does Graham ever miss his first love – music? 'One has certainly fed the other. All adjectives that you use in music can be applied to the garden: rhythm, harmony, movement, cadences, colour, punctuation. I sometimes think that my sense of phrasing when singing was learnt early on from the downland profile I grew up with as a child. The curves of the Downs are full of tension and rhythm, just like music.'

Graham is generous in his acknowledgement of those who have influenced and helped him along the way. Lucy is always an inspiration and her artist's sense of colour and texture has added much to the garden at Marchants. He pays homage to the horticultural experience of Sibylle Kreutsberger and Pam Schwerdt: 'they taught me to be absolutely rigorous when selecting plants'. Christopher Lloyd (see p. 54) taught him 'objectivity and to be your own person, to stand on your own with your own thinking'. By way of thanks, at Lloyd's 80th birthday party Graham sang Schumann's *Dichterliebe* for him and Lucy presented him with a tie she had made, based on the colours of his long border!

## Marchants' magic

The nursery at Marchants offers a wide range of plants including herbaceous perennials, grasses, shrubs, alpines and bulbs. They specialise in the genera agapanthus, galanthus, miscanthus and sedum and Graham has raised many fine varieties. These are just a few:

🌺 *Agapanthus 'Marchants' Cobalt Cracker'*, a much-admired vibrant colbalt blue form, selected in 2004.

🌺 *Agapanthus 'Quink Drops'*, as its title suggests this plant drips dazzling buds of the deepest purple blue.

🌺 *Erodium 'Marchants' Mikado'*, a remarkably striking storksbill whose lilac pink flowers are marked with a pair of black flashing eyes on the upper petals.

🌺 *Hemerocallis 'Laughton Tower'*, bred specifically for height, to grow among tall grasses and reaching up to a metre and a half. It has apricot orange flowers.

🌺 *Lithodora 'Star'*, a blue and white sport (the term for a plant that shows a marked variation from its parent), spotted by Graham while he was mowing the lawn at Washfield Nursery.

🌺 *Sedum 'Purple Emperor'*, of this dramatic plant with deep matt foliage and sturdy habit, garden writer Val Bourne wrote that it is 'often quoted as the finest dark variety of all… the whole plant has great poise and balance'.

🌺 *Sedum 'Red Cauli'*, a seedling selected at Marchants. Bluish-grey foliage with small cauliflower-like clusters of ruby red flowers, hence its name.

🌺 *Sedum 'Marchants' Best Red'*, a beautiful variety, green foliage, purple flushed with rich wine red flowers, arguably the darkest of any sedum. All these sedums have earned the RHS's accolade of 'Award of Garden Merit'.

**Top Place**
🔘 *Marchants Hardy Plants, tel. 01323 811737*

# ARTHUR HELLYER
## *1902-93*

Anyone who regularly browses the gardening shelves of their local library or second-hand bookshop will be familiar with the name Arthur Hellyer. A prolific writer, he authored over 30 books and contributed to or edited many more, along with literally hundreds of magazine articles and features. He lived and gardened in Sussex for almost 60 years and deserves to be remembered as an influential educator and invaluable guide for professional and amateur gardeners alike.

Arthur George Lee Hellyer was born in Bristol but grew up in London, attending Dulwich College. After leaving school in 1917 Arthur was advised to seek work outdoors due to a respiratory condition. His father was state's auditor for Jersey and Arthur worked first at a Guernsey tomato farm, then transferred to a farm on Jersey. However, most of his horticultural knowledge was gained back in Bristol where he moved following his father's death in 1921. Here he worked as a nurseryman with a wide range of plant species and by 1930 was well regarded as an accomplished plantsman.

By this time, Arthur had already begun disseminating his considerable practical knowledge through periodicals. In 1929 he became assistant editor of *Commercial Horticulture*, then took up the same post at *Amateur Gardening*. His magazine career was now well established. By 1946 he was editor of *Amateur Gardener*, a position he remained in until his retirement 21 years later. Under his editorship circulation reached a staggering high of 300,000 copies a week. He was also editing *Gardening Illustrated* during this period. Even after his 'official' retirement Arthur's written output was prodigious, contributing numerous articles to magazines and periodicals such as *The Garden*, *Country Life* and *Homes and Gardens*, as well as acting as the weekly gardening correspondent for the *Financial Times*.

Arthur's first book was *Practical Gardening for Amateurs* published in 1935. It was the first of many and his books always sold well; for instance, his *Popular Encyclopaedia of Flowering Plants* (1957) went into 23 editions. Subjects also covered include garden history, design and horticultural exhibiting. He was a great champion of garden visiting, as well as an enthusiastic and accomplished photographer. Most of Arthur's practical advice is as relevant for the modern-day gardener as it was for his contemporaries with the big exception of his use of chemicals – 'organic' was not part of his vocabulary! Many of the substances he advocated using have been deemed so potent that they are no longer available. Times do indeed change and not always for the worse.

Although Arthur's prose is unlikely to ever set the reader on fire, it is always clear, precise and instructive. The reader definitely feels  in a safe pair of hands when seeking advice from one of his books. Certainly, this is gardening of the old school, no 48-hour makeovers for him. In the introduction to *Designing and Planting Your Garden*, a 1986 reprint of a book originally published in 1935 (not many 50-year-old practical books achieve a reprint!), Arthur addresses the new gardener with encouragement but offers no promise of a quick fix.

> *Whether a garden has to be made from the chaos left by the builder or from an existing garden that does not match one's taste or requirements, it is usually wise to take one's time over it. That is why I have divided the chapters of this book into three sections, the first two each representing a year's work and the third dealing with some of the maintenance work that is necessary in any garden.*[1]

1. *Hellyer, A.G.L.,* Designing and Planting Your Garden, *Hamlyn, Twickenham, 1986, p.6.*

With faint encouragement, he acknowledges that the process can be quickened, 'though I do not think that "instant gardens" are, in the long term, usually the best gardens, they are a possibility.'[2]

Perhaps it is the very thoroughness of Arthur's approach and his unwillingness to take short cuts that made him stick with the printed medium rather than branching out into television or radio. I am sure the offers must have come as his extensive knowledge, coupled with his ability as a communicator and teacher, would have made him a prime candidate for broadcasting. He is reported to have had a quiet and retiring manner so perhaps was not temperamentally disposed to life in the spotlight, though one should not gain the impression that he was afraid to express strong opinions. For instance, he questioned the view that the 18th-century English landscape garden was the highest achievement of our garden making, and certainly felt it was not what the ordinary garden visitor most relished.

> What they [the garden visitor] enjoy is something totally different. It is the far more cosy inward-looking gardens of our own century; gardens which have been conceived as environments for people and plants and which are full of flowers and foliage for much of the year. Yet this kind of flowery garden has been almost entirely the concern of amateurs and has earned little approval from the top professional designers, most of whom regard it as sentimental and disorganised. Perhaps this is just another example of the ever widening gap between experts and the general public. However, even if this is so it does not follow that the professionals are right and the amateurs are wrong.[3]

Arthur married Grace Bolt (known to all as Gay) in 1933 and they had two boys and a girl. Gay was a knowledgeable botanist and gardener and their marriage appears to have been a loving and enduring partnership; she is also reported to have been a mean indexer and proof reader. The year following their marriage, Arthur and Gay moved to a plot of farmland at Rowfant, a hamlet between East Grinstead and Crawley, which became known as 'Orchards'. Here, on their 8.5 acres

2. Hellyer, A.G.L., Designing and Planting Your Garden, Hamlyn, Twickenham, 1986, p.6.
3. Hellyer, A.G.L., Gardens of Genius, Hamlyn, London, 1980, p.6.

(3.4 hectares) they set about building a wooden shack, followed by a house they literally built themselves in the style of a Canadian barn and, most importantly, creating a beautiful wooded garden. During and after World War II Orchards was run as a market garden, supplying produce from productive apple and pear orchards and large fruit and vegetable gardens. Cows and goats were also resident at this time, all contributors to the war effort. After the closure of the market garden, Arthur and Gay remained at Orchards and continued to develop and enjoy the garden as a purely private space. They shared a passion for ornamental trees and planted plenty, many of which are now mature specimens and have been registered as trees of national importance.

Needless to say, such was his acknowledged expertise that Arthur was a very active member of the RHS, acting both as its Vice-President and as a judge on the floral committee. They awarded him the Victoria Medal of Honour and the Dean Hole Medal. He was made a fellow of the Linnean Society and in 1967 he was awarded a much-deserved MBE for his services to horticulture. Sadly, Gay died in 1977; Arthur remained at Orchards, continuing to garden, greatly assisted by his daughter Penelope, until only a few months before his own death. It is perhaps fitting that Arthur's final days were spent in the nursing home at Henfield, run by the Gardeners' Royal Benevolent Society (now known as Perennial), a charity he had long championed and supported.

**Top Works & Place**
- Popular Encyclopaedia of Flowering Plants, *1957*
- Your Garden Week by Week, *1936*
- Shell Guide to Gardens, *editor, 1977*
- *Orchards, Rowfant*

# DEREK JARMAN
## 1942-94

Yes, yes, I know Derek Jarman was actually a *Kent* gardener and not a Sussex one but his completely innovative and original garden at Prospect Cottage, Dungeness, has had such an enduring influence on coastal gardens all along the south coast, that I feel quite justified in including him here. So often we need artists to show us the beauty that can be found in unexpected places, and Derek revealed the beauty of this desolate and very particular windswept corner of Kent. Overshadowed by its looming nuclear power station, Dungeness is now much sought after not just by traditional fishermen but also by smart weekenders.

Derek Jarman was a true polymath, excelling in many fields. *The Literary Encyclopedia* lists him as 'Autobiographer, Diarist, Film Maker, Painter, Polemicist, Political Activist, Scriptwriter' (yet, interestingly, not as Gardener). Derek studied at King's College, London, then at the Slade School of Art. His early career included designing sets and costumes for productions by the choreographer Frederick Ashton and working alongside the film-maker Ken Russell. His paintings were exhibited widely and he was a Turner Prize nominee in 1986. Among his best revered films are *Caravaggio* (1986), *The Last of England* (1988) and *War Requiem* (1989). Derek was a high profile public activist for gay rights and for AIDS, the disease that sadly claimed him in his early 50s. For more information on his work, I recommend the Slow Motion

Angel website devoted to what they term Derek's 'beautiful, enriching, oppositional and challenging' work (*www.slowmotionangel.com*).

Derek had been a keen gardener from childhood but when he bought Prospect Cottage in the mid-1980s, surrounded by shingle and sea, he had no plans for creating a garden in such an unlikely setting. He was first tempted to begin to shape the immediate landscape around the cottage using a collection of flints he had picked up on his shoreline walks.

> *I decided to stop there; after all, the bleakness of Prospect Cottage was what had made me fall in love with it. At the back I planted a dog rose. Then I found a curious piece of driftwood and used this, and one of the necklaces of holey stones that I hung on the wall to stake the rose. The garden had begun.*[1]

Thus were the early stirrings of a garden that was to spawn hundreds of imitations. Although some are undoubtedly far more successful than others, the real contribution the Dungeness garden has made is to show this generation of gardeners a new way of looking at a plot, a new way to view the plants we grow and the way we integrate them into our surroundings.

Gradually, a low-growing oasis of colour, texture and movement, punctuated by strong forms began to take shape around Prospect Cottage, a simple single-storey abode stained the deepest black with the brightest orange windows and door. Derek drew formal, geometric shapes on the ground constructed from irregular and uniquely shaped pebbles, stones and flint. Incorporated into this low-lying moonscape were strong vertical accents made from driftwood and discarded and rusted tools and implements. Pockets of soil between these structures became the unlikely homes for a huge variety of plants, carefully chosen to suit these dry, windy and salt-laden conditions, and all thrived (many purchased from Elizabeth Strangman's Washfield Nursery at Hawkhurst). Cotton lavender, poppies, sea kale, gorse, cistus and marigolds became Derek's signature plants, augmented by herbs, bulbs and many more. He even grew vegetables in raised beds and had a

---

1. Jarman, Derek, Derek Jarman's Garden, *Thames & Hudson, London, 1995, p.12.*

productive beehive. He had created a garden without a lawn, something he held in the highest contempt as this comment reveals: 'For the same trouble of mowing, you could have a year's vegetables: runner beans, cauliflowers and cabbages, mixed with pinks and peonies, Shirley poppies and delphiniums, wouldn't that beautify the land and save us from the garden terrorism that prevails?'[2]

Derek Jarman's garden thankfully survives and flourishes and is as lasting a testament to his creativity and imagination as his achievements in the fields of film-making and painting. Yet this precious jewel is set within a fragile and public environment and the stir it created has inevitably and naturally led to an influx of visitors to the area. Perhaps not all are as sensitive as they could be both to the fragility of the site or to the privacy of those for whom this extraordinary bit of England is home. I urge visitors to tread with care or indeed to enjoy the garden instead, and its creator's writing, through the wonderful book *Derek Jarman's Garden*, illustrated with Howard Sooley's stunning and evocative photographs. This is a beautiful, challenging and exciting garden created in the most unlikely of settings and yet wholly appropriate to its surroundings which, surely, must always be the highest achievement of any gardener.

> *Here at the sea's edge*
>   *I have planted my dragon-toothed garden*
> *to defend the porch,*
>     *steadfast warriors*
> *against those who protest their impropriety*
>   *even to the end of the world.*

**DEREK JARMAN**
*DEREK JARMAN'S GARDEN, 1995*

---

**1.** *Jarman, Derek,* Derek Jarman's Garden, *Thames & Hudson, London, 1995, p.7.*

**Top Works & Place**
- Caravaggio, *1986*
- War Requiem, *1989*
- *Prospect Cottage, Dungeness*

# RUDYARD KIPLING
## *1865 - 1936*

Along with Hilaire Belloc and Virginia Woolf, Rudyard Kipling is one of the writers most readily associated with Sussex. He was also an enthusiastic gardener and garden designer and it is still possible today to visit the gardens of his two former homes in the county. He rented The Elms on the village green at Rottingdean from 1897 to 1902. Although he was fond of the village, the house became infused with bitter sadness after the death of his daughter Josephine, aged six, in 1899. His discomfort and distress was further exacerbated by his loss of privacy. Frequently 'admirers' would hang from the upper deck of horse-drawn buses driven close alongside his high garden walls, straining to catch a glimpse of the famous writer tending his garden. Not surprisingly, Rudyard and his wife Carrie began to look for a more peaceful Sussex retreat. Much of the former garden of The Elms is now owned and beautifully tended by the local council, open to the public throughout the year and well worth a visit.

For Rudyard rescue from such unwelcome intrusions came in the form of a beautifully mellow 17th-century sandstone house called Bateman's, to the south of Burwash in the Sussex Weald. The Kiplings, with their surviving children John and Elsie, moved here in September 1902. Shortly afterwards, Rudyard wrote to his long-time friend Charles Eliot Norton: 'England is a wonderful land. It is the most marvellous of all foreign countries I have ever been in. It is made up of trees and green fields and mud and the gentry, and at last I'm one of the gentry.'[1] This extract is typical of a letter full of the enthusiasm and pride commonly found among new house owners yet is tellingly tinged with a sense of irony, as Rudyard could never convincingly be 'one of the gentry', nor indeed did he wish to be. Yet, despite the self-mocking tone, it does seem that he had finally found a corner of England to call his own and here he settled for the rest of his life.

The house, garden and surrounding countryside exude a calm and restraint that must have been a welcome contrast to the increasingly hectic seaside atmosphere from which he had fled. Nathaniel Lloyd (see p.54) wrote of the garden at Bateman's: 'There is nothing fussy, nothing showy, nothing savouring of the villa, not even a flower bed. There is none of the shopkeeper's desire to dress the front as if it were a shop window.'[2] Of the garden as it appears today Rudyard's main design input was the pond area, the walled Mulberry Garden and the Pear Arch. The latter was built to his design and is a long alley formed from the generous spread of iron arches that support a variety of espaliered pear trees. It terminates in an attractive brickwork seat. The arch aligns with the entrance to the Mulberry Garden, although the original eponymous tree planted by the writer in 1905 has been replaced with a much younger specimen. He transformed this former wagon yard into a pretty walled enclosure, using old millstones to articulate the main path.

On display in the house is Rudyard's 1906 ink and watercolour sketch for the Pond and Rose Garden. He earmarked the proceeds (£7,700) of his 1907 Nobel Prize money for the development of this area. His main concern was to create a safe place for children to boat and swim, complete with a 6-foot (2-metre) skiff with hand-cranked paddle-wheels. One of his main pleasures in life was the company of children and he enthusiastically took part in even the most boisterous of games. The sundial set within a semi-circular niche of yew hedging bordering the formal Rose Garden bears the legend 'it is later than you think'.

---

**1.** *Kipling, Rudyard, Letter to C.E. Norton, November 3rd 1902.*
**2.** *Lloyd, Nathaniel, 1919, quoted by Adam Nicolson in* Bateman's, *National Trust, 2004, p.28.*

Carrie claimed her husband would show this to visitors whom he began to feel had outstayed their welcome!

Rudyard may have had some impressive professional advice on the layout of the garden but the documentation is tantalisingly flimsy. On August 3rd 1906 an entry in the Visitors' Book notes: 'To lunch Mr Robinson. Suggests alterations in the garden.' We can only speculate that this could have been the garden doyen William Robinson (*see p.65*). Certainly Rudyard was not one who confined his gardening activities to making plans with pen and paper and directing others to dig and hoe, as a letter to a friend illustrates.

> *Yesterday (these are the things one really works for) the wife and I had a glorious day in the garden alone … building a little dry stone wall to the edge of a bed which had long been an eyesore. We knocked off, stiff, sore (stones aren't easy to handle), pretty dirty, but quite happy. Why is it that one gets more joy over a job like this than 'literature'?* [3]

Such enthusiastic eulogising suggests they were far from daunted by the physical and theoretical practicalities of garden and farm. Among the books that line Rudyard's study walls are *Talks on Manures* along with *Fences, Gates and Bridges*, while on a less prosaic note his constant companion was C.A. John's *Flowers of the Field*.

Rudyard not only busied himself in the garden at Bateman's but also saw himself as something of an agriculturalist. When he bought the estate it came with a modest 33 acres (13.4 hectares), which he increased to 300 acres (121.4 hectares) over the years. In practice, Carrie proved to be the better farmer, directing the running of the estate, while her husband was more suited to the garden. Of course, they also employed several gardeners and were supportive of Viscountess Wolseley's scheme to train women in horticulture (*see p.80*). However, domestic propriety seems to have hampered this plan, as noted by Rudyard in a letter to Wolseley: '…Mrs Kipling very seriously thinks of having women gardeners, only she is abashed at the difficulties of housing them.' [4]

3. *Kipling, Rudyard, Letter to Andrew Macphail, June 25th 1910.*
4. *Kipling, Rudyard, Letter to Frances Wolseley, May 29th 1915.*

Certainly, nice young ladies couldn't be billeted in the bothy with the men, although during wartime the farm was run 'on a sprinkling of female labour'.[5]

Sadly, family tragedy once again visited the Kiplings in their rural idyll. In September 1915, their son John was reported missing on the first day of action at the Battle of Loos, dealing the loving parents a second, unbearable blow. Apart from the company of visitors, the couple lived on rather alone at Bateman's, especially after their daughter Elsie left to marry in 1924. Rudyard died in 1936 and Carrie lived for another three years. In a final act of generosity, she bequeathed the house, along with the garden her husband had loved so much, to the National Trust.

> Our England is a garden that is full of stately views,
>     Of borders, beds and shrubberies and lawns and avenues,
> With statues on the terraces and peacocks strutting by;
>     But the Glory of the Garden lies in more than meets the eye.
>
> For where the old thick laurels grow, along the thin red wall,
>     You will find the tool- and potting-sheds which are the heart of all;
> The cold-frames and the hot-houses, the dungpits and the tanks,
>     The rollers, carts and drainpipes, with the barrows and the planks.
>
> And there you'll see the gardeners, the men and 'prentice boys
>     Told off to do as they are bid and do it without noise;
> For, except when seeds are planted and we shout to scare the birds,
>     The Glory of the Garden it abideth not in words.

**RUDYARD KIPLING**
EXTRACT FROM *THE GLORY OF THE GARDEN*

---

**5.** *Kipling, Rudyard, quoted by David Gilmour in* The Long Recessional, *Pimlico, London, 2003, p.283.*

**Top Work & Places**

❯ The Glory of the Garden, *1911*

❯ *Bateman's, Burwash, tel. 01435 882302, website: www.nationaltrust.org.uk*

❯ *Kipling Gardens, Rottingdean, tel. 01273 292059, website: www.brighton-hove.gov.uk*

# NATHANIEL & CHRISTOPHER LLOYD
## *1867-1933 & 1921-2006*

No garden visitor to the southern counties of England should omit Great Dixter from their tour, it is as essential as Sissinghurst. Here we have a rare example of gardening continuity and commitment, from 1910 to the present day and from father to son. But let such longevity in no way suggest stagnation as the gardens at Dixter are synonymous worldwide with change and innovation.

The arrangement of buildings and the main garden layout are the legacy of Nathaniel Lloyd. This mellow classic English backdrop of generous tiled roofs, sheltering eaves and 'ancient' topiary belies the early origins of their creator, for Nathaniel was far from aristocratic, indeed he was very much 'in trade'. Born to a wealthy middle-class family in Manchester, after overseeing the advertising and printing for the Mazzawatte Tea Company he founded his own lithographic printers in 1893. Nathaniel was able to retire in his early 40s and indulge his passions for golf, shooting and antique furniture. By this time he had married Daisy Field, a union destined to produce six children.

When Nathaniel purchased the Dixter estate in 1910 (the 'Great' was only added post expansion), it comprised the portion of the original 15th-century house built *in situ*. He approached Edwin Lutyens (*see p.91*), to propose restoration and expansion plans. Nathaniel very much shared Lutyens' respect and admiration for local vernacular building traditions. At Lutyens' suggestion, the shambling remains of a 16th-century timber-framed house were purchased for £75, then transported from Benenden. After careful re-erection and sensitive integration alongside the earlier existing house, this formed the Yeoman's Hall. As all who visit today can see, it was done with consummate skill and respect; this is certainly no heavy-handed pastiche of merry old England. As Nathaniel wrote: 'The spirit in which the work has been done may be summed up by saying that nothing has been done without authority, nothing has been done from imagination; there has been no forgery.'[1]

Such was the enthusiasm for the restoration of his new estate that Nathaniel developed something of a second career as an architect and building historian, becoming a Fellow of the Royal Institute of British Architects in 1931. He restored Higham at Northiam and published several respected books, including *A History of the English House* (1931), and *A History of English Brickwork* (1934). However, he was also a very keen gardener and, although much of the layout of the yew hedges at Great Dixter conform to Lutyens' original garden plans, Nathaniel was responsible for the topiary. His 1923 book *Garden Craftsmanship in Yew and Box* is still in print today. As his son later commented: 'The apparent antiquity of the yew hedges is spurious. All, as well as the topiary, in which my father was particularly interested, were planted 1912 or later.'[2] Nathaniel also designed the Sunk Garden, a former lawn that was turned over to vegetables during World War I. After the hostilities ended he is reported as saying, 'Now we can play.'

Lloyd senior is responsible for the material structure of Great Dixter, but Christopher really put it on the map. Youngest of Nathaniel and Daisy's large family, Christopher was deeply influenced by his mother from an early age. She was a knowledgeable plantswoman and avid follower of William Robinson (*see p.65*). It is interesting to note that the spirit of Christopher's book *The Mixed Border* (1957), very much chimes with Robinson's 1871 classic *Hardy Flowers* and it was Daisy who first introduced the beautiful flowering meadows to the garden.

**1.** *Lloyd, Nathaniel, unpublished memorandum, c.1913, quoted in* A Guide to Great Dixter, *Lloyd, Christopher and Hind, Charles, 2006, p.3.*
**2.** *Ibid., Lloyd, Christopher, p.9.*

Christopher was educated at Rugby College, he studied French and German at Cambridge then did his stint of National Service. At Wye College he studied horticulture and became an assistant lecturer teaching decorative horticulture there from 1950 to 1954. He then returned home and ran the nursery and eventually the whole garden at Dixter, where he stayed until his death, aged 84. He was a recipient of the RHS Victoria Medal of Honour as well as gaining an OBE in 2000. Gertrude Jekyll (see p. 90) visited Christopher's parents at Great Dixter in the 1920s and he remembered her saying to his young self, 'I hope you'll grow up to be a great gardener', which of course he did.

I do not think it an overstatement to say that Christopher Lloyd revolutionised the way many British gardeners used colour in their gardens in the latter part of the 20th century. And, perhaps more surprisingly, his signature use of exotic forms such as cannas, yuccas and banana plants has been eagerly adopted in numerous municipally managed spaces, from public parks to traffic roundabouts. He rejected the safe, time-worn subtleties of white, mauve and grey in his borders, threw away the colour wheel and let the sun shine on every possible colour combination and hue, the more unlikely the better! This approach to using colour is perhaps eloquent of his enthusiastic zest for life; not just for gardening but for opera, food, travelling, writing and above all for his friends (who always addressed him as 'Christo'). Lloyd junior was also among the great plantsmen of his generation. Yet his inexhaustive horticultural knowledge and curiosity about the habitat, form and variety of plants never detracted from his unique sense of design.

Today the gardens at Dixter are still a riot of bold colour and exciting forms, and all is executed with the highest standard of plantsmanship and horticultural excellence. Christopher may have been something of a gardening iconoclast but he was never anarchic. Not for him the ease of labour-saving ground cover; Great Dixter is a high, high-maintenance garden in which only the most elevated standards were, and indeed are, tolerated. In an interview in the 1990s, he asserted: 'I've always said that a high-maintenance garden is the most interesting.' And part of that interest is achieved through change and innovation.

'There are too many people who get stuck in a rut and hark back to the past all the time and talk about conservation for lack of new ideas of their own. It's easier to copy than create.'[3] As he asserted in the preface to probably his best-loved book, 'Effort is only troublesome when you are bored. *The Well-Tempered Garden* is for gardeners who have not been dragged into this pursuit but are here because they love it.'[4]

Christopher was a prolific writer, known to many through his numerous books and his columns in the *Observer*, *Guardian* and *Country Life*. His writing, like his conversation, was always lively, informative and opinionated. To friends and strangers alike he could in turns be charming and exceedingly rude. He did not suffer fools gladly nor court favour. In the guide he wrote to Great Dixter he rather exhaustively lists from points one to nine why he does not label the plants in his borders. The following selection gives something of the flavour of the man:

> 2. I hate the look of labels. Like a cemetery... 5. It is easier to pop a label into a handbag than to try and memorise it on the spot... 9. Even when plants are clearly labelled the public will still ask their name if anyone is around to talk to. They're on an outing. We're trying to work.[5]

Despite (or more likely because of) his forthright character, Christopher Lloyd was greatly mourned, publicly and privately, when he died in early 2006. In his latter years he had established The Great Dixter Charitable Trust, dedicated to maintaining, conserving and enhancing his unique house and garden. With the skilful guidance of head gardener Fergus Garrett (*see p.88*) and his team, the garden looks set to continue to thrive under its third generation of committed custodians.

---

**3.** *Lloyd, Christopher, 'Horticultural Who's Who' in* Gardens Illustrated, *Dec.-Jan. 1993-94, p.62.*
**4.** *Lloyd, Christopher,* The Well-Tempered Garden, *Weidenfeld & Nicolson, London, 2003, preface.*
**5.** *Lloyd, Christopher, A Guide to Great Dixter, 2006, p.17.*

**Nathaniel Lloyd's Top Work**
❯ Garden Craftsmanship in Yew and Box, *1923*

**Christopher Lloyd's Top Place & Works**
❯ The Well-Tempered Garden, *1970*
❯ In My Garden, *1993*
❯ *Great Dixter, Northiam, tel. 01797 252878, website: www.greatdixter.co.uk*

# SIR GERALD LODER & FAMILY
## 1861-1936

Sir Gerald Walter Erskine Loder is perhaps the best known member of what is undoubtedly something of an exceptional Sussex gardening dynasty. Sir Gerald's legacy is the great garden at Wakehurst Place, now managed by the Royal Botanic Gardens, Kew but other notable Sussex gardens, The High Beeches and Leonardslee, also have strong Loder connections.

Gerald's father, Sir Robert Loder, acquired The High Beeches estate at Handcross in 1847. Gerald spent his early years there and at Whittlebury in Northamptonshire, his family's other estate. He read Law at Trinity College, Cambridge, and was called to the Bar in 1888. A keen politician, Gerald served as MP for Brighton from 1889 to 1906 and was active at government level for many years. Much later, in 1934, he became a peer, taking the title Lord Wakehurst of Ardingly. Although a keen sportsman, playing golf (he had practice golf tees incorporated into the layout of Wakehurst), cricket and that most gentlemanly of games, real tennis, Gerald's enduring passion was plants and gardening but on a very grand scale indeed.

In 1903, Gerald bought the Wakehurst Place estate with a house that was originally built by a distant antecedent of Nicholas Culpeper (*see p.87*) and dates back to 1590. Gerald had a special interest in the plants of eastern Asia, South America, Australia and New Zealand and he set about building up a fine and extensive collection, sponsoring many of the great plant-hunters of the day, including Kingdon-Ward, Comber and Forrest. A particular passion was conifers and he developed a plantation known as The Pinetum. Rhododendrons are a feature of the grounds at Wakehurst, although he always favoured the species over hybrid varieties.

Key to the success of the gardens at Wakehurst Place was Gerald's head gardener, Alfred Coates. A much-quoted story is told about Coates's interview for the post, which was conducted at the House of Lords in London. Gerald is said to have asked: 'Well, Coates, what shall it be; flowers, or trees and shrubs?' The reply came quickly and decisively, 'I reckon trees and shrubs, sir.' Thus was decided the future fate of what was to become one of England's great gardens and plant collections. The contribution and skill of Alfred Coates is recognised today in the inscription on the sundial in the area of the garden known as The Slips. It is some lines by the poet J.G. Whittier which I feel are a fitting memorial to all the gardeners in this book.

> Give fools their gold and knaves their power,
>     Let fortunes' bubbles rise and fall,
>   Who sows a field or trains a flower,
>       Or plants a tree, is more than all

Throughout the years of Gerald's and Coates's stewardship of the gardens at Wakehurst, huge numbers of plants would arrive regularly from nurseries at home and abroad, while seeds were sent from foreign expeditions. Gerald always insisted on being present when these exciting packages were opened. He kept meticulous records of his plants and these invaluable notebooks are now housed at Kew. As early as 1908, his *Catalogue of Trees, Shrubs etc., at Wakehurst Place, Sussex* noted some 3,000 species and cultivars. Great pains were always taken to place new plants in the most auspicious position on the estate. To this end it was a common sight to see Gerald striding across his grounds, followed by a garden boy pushing a plant-filled wheelbarrow, searching for just the right place for the new arrival. He firmly believed that 'any plant worth seeing is worth walking to'. Once in the ground, plants received ongoing and attentive care, thus ensuring they thrived.

However, Gerald's role in the garden was far from one of mere direction and instruction, he could be quite 'hands-on', though not always with the best results. During his weekend stays in Sussex he would prowl the estate armed with secateurs and a saw. Once 'the master' was safely back in London, Coates and a garden boy would spend their Monday mornings rectifying any damage! As might be suspected, his attitude to indoor flowers was somewhat lukewarm; he favoured a single specimen bloom displayed in a vase rather than the bountiful and extravagant floral displays commonly found in grand country houses. His garden staff was told in no uncertain terms that they were employed to grow trees and shrubs, not violets for the table. Apart from Wakehurst and politics, Gerald led a full and active public life. He was a member of county archaeological and antiquarian societies, President of the Royal Arboricultural Society, Vice-President of the Linnaean Society and President of the Royal Horticultural Society. He also held the prestigious Victoria Medal of Honour from the RHS.

After Gerald's death in 1936, Wakehurst Place was bought by Sir Henry Price and his wife Lady Eve (see p.91) who continued to develop the gardens. Price bequeathed it to the National Trust who now leases it to the Royal Botanic Gardens. Its favourable climate, high rainfall and excellent soil allow the growth of many plants that do not do well at Kew Gardens. The estate now extends to 465 acres (188 hectares) and is home to National Collections of birches, hypericums, skimmias and southern birches. The splendid Millennium Seed Bank, which aims to conserve biodiversity by storing the seeds of 24,000 plant species, can also be found here. It is a venture I am sure Sir Gerald Loder would have wholeheartedly supported.

The gardening gene ran deep within the extended Loder family. Gerald's brother Reginald is known to have made a beautiful garden at his home Maidwell Hall in Northamptonshire, while the eldest brother, Sir Edmund, acquired that other great Sussex garden, Leonardslee, in 1889. He was a keen hybridiser of rhododendrons. His son Robert inherited the garden on his death as in turn did his son, Sir Giles. Giles continued the family horticultural tradition, being a great RHS supporter, exhibitor and award winner. It was during his stewardship of Leonardslee that the garden was used as the setting for the 1947 film *Black Narcissus*, as it was considered to present such a convincing picture of the Himalayas! At the time of writing, the gardens are up for sale, so seem destined to leave the Loder family. However, let's hope they long remain home to the descendants of the wonderful wallabies that were first introduced by Sir Edmund.

## The Rhododendron Loderi Group

Any gardener who grows rhododendrons will be familiar with the name Loderi. In 1901 Sir Edmund Loder at Leonardslee crossed *Rhododendron griffithainum* with *R. fortunei* and created *R. loderi*. This grows into a large, beautiful, evergreen plant, smothered in white to pink blooms in May time. The cross gave birth to the Rhododendron Loderi Group that is considered to contain the very best hybrids in England (though sadly many did not bloom until after Sir Edmund's death in 1920). Of the numerous subsequent cultivars, many cite *R. Loderi* 'King George' to be the finest and it has received the RHS Award of Garden Merit, as have *R. Loderi* 'Game Chick', *R. Loderi* 'Pink Diamond', *R. Loderi* 'Pink Topaz' and *R. Loderi* 'Venus'. All have large fragrant blooms borne in open trusses comprising between nine to 12 individual flowers that are pink when in bud, but open to reveal varying shades from white to pink, depending on type.

In memory of his brother Edmund, Sir Gerald Loder (Lord Wakehurst) instituted the Loder Rhododendron Cup in 1921. This silver-gilt Challenge Cup was made to an ancient Irish design and was fittingly awarded to Edmund's grandson Giles in 1997 for his outstanding work on the species. Giles Loder was also an RHS Gold Medal winner and in 1967 was awarded the prestigious Victoria Medal of Honour, thus continuing a family tradition.

**Top Places**

❯ *Wakehurst Place, tel. 01444 894066, website: www.kew.org.uk*
❯ *Leonardslee, tel. 01403 891212, website: www.leonardsleegardens.com*
❯ *The High Beeches, tel. 01444 400589, website: www.highbeeches.com*

# SARAH RAVEN
*born 1963*

Any book about inspiring Sussex gardeners has to include Sarah Raven as she is the motivator *par excellence* to the new, inexperienced or simply rather jaded gardener. As a teacher, her approach is very much that of learning through doing, having some fun and above all creating something that is visually beautiful. Sarah is passionate about gardening, as she is about cooking, but the message is that these are passions that should enhance one's life, not become yet another chore.

After initially reading history at university Sarah changed direction, studied medicine and began her doctor's training at the Royal Sussex County Hospital in Brighton. However, the birth of her second daughter highlighted the incompatibility of the medic's life with motherhood. Earlier, while first on maternity leave, Sarah had started a contract florist business in London with a friend. The lack of interesting floral material at the wholesale markets led Sarah to investigate growing her own and she was somewhat surprised at the paucity of information available on growing annuals. It seemed that no one any longer grew this most easy and diverse group of plants to fill their homes with beautiful and inexpensive blooms. After much trial and error and a time spent as a volunteer at Great Dixter, Sarah was in a position to write her first book, *The Cutting Garden*. Published in 1996, it promptly won the Garden Writers' Guild Award for Best Specialist Gardening Book and is responsible for a renaissance in the domestic growing of flowers for cutting.

During this period Sarah and her husband, the writer Adam Nicolson, had moved from London to a farm called Perch Hill, set deep within a lovely wooded Sussex valley. They were fired with the idea of keeping animals and growing some of their food here. It also provided the perfect venue for the growing and flower-arranging courses Sarah was now running, and for her mail order business supplying seeds and plants. Such was the success of the courses (soon expanded to include other related topics) that more space was needed. Thus the beautiful, and functional, 'greenhouse' building was conceived and constructed. Inspired by the Amsterdam restaurant De Kas, the 490 sq. foot (150 sq. metre) glass structure is now home to her school. Inside, flowers, salads and vegetables grow in raised beds, boxes and pots, jostling for position alongside garden implements and the students' chairs and tables. If only all schoolrooms could look like this! More books have followed and Sarah became a regular contributor to BBC television's *Gardeners' World*, further spreading her infectious enthusiasm and knowledge to a wider audience – all quite impressive for someone with no formal horticultural training.

When I met Sarah at Perch Hill we discussed who had influenced and inspired her. Her father, a university don, was a keen botanist and Sarah spent many happy childhood hours with him observing and collecting plants in the wild. Her mother was a passionate gardener both in Cambridge, where Sarah grew up, and in the contrasting conditions of the western coast of Scotland, where they spent their family summers. Christopher Lloyd (*see p. 54*) was also a great source of knowledge and visual inspiration. Her co-presenter on *Gardeners' World*, Monty Don, she first met through her husband, as they are old friends. Don and Sarah continue to share and swap gardening expertise and he too has no formal horticultural education. Both are largely self-taught and possess a very strong and original visual sense which they apply freely to their gardens. Each believes that gardens should be productive but beautiful places too.

Even the most cursory glance at Sarah's *Kitchen & Garden* catalogue shows that herbs and vegetables are quite as important to her as flowers. 'From my interest in growing annuals the move towards raising vegetables from seed was inevitable. Flowers are a luxury but food a necessity.' The group of plants that converted her were the easy-to-grow, cut-and-come-again varieties of salad leaves and these are the ones she advises all novices to begin with. 'Modern life is so busy that many people don't have time to grow and harvest much. I am not dictatorial in my teaching – I think you should do what you can.' Likewise she is not impressed by what she calls 'anally retentive food'; time spent in Italy taught her the importance of the freshest food prepared simply and quickly.

Sarah has always cooked and finds it 'companionable and relaxing. I love learning new things and cooking has a slow, meandering learning curve'. She cites Elizabeth David, Jane Grigson and Nigel Slater as writers whose approach she finds stimulating. Constance Spry was another formative influence. Now most remembered for what were then considered her rather avant-garde floral arrangements, Spry also published a best-selling cookery book. Sarah says she owes much to Rose Gray. As a student she worked as a waitress at Gray's River Café in London where the ethos was to involve the front-of-house staff in the preparation of the food, giving them a proper understanding of what they were serving. She now takes a similar approach at the school, encouraging her cooks to create meals from what they can harvest there. Likewise her cookery book *Sarah Raven's Garden Cookbook* (2007), largely arose from the food that is served at the school. Needless to say, if not actually grown or raised on the farm, everything is sourced locally.

Sarah's husband Adam is the grandson of Vita Sackville-West and, following the death of his father Nigel in 2004, has the tenancy of a house on the Sissinghurst estate in neighbouring Kent (owned by the National Trust). Part of the Raven/Nicolson family's time is now spent there and they are involved in a project to grow on the estate the food that will be served at the Trust's restaurant. However, Perch Hill, with its inspiring and lovely garden, remains very much the family home.

**Top Works & Place**

❯ *Perch Hill Farm, near Brightling, tel. 0845 0504849, website: www.perchhill.co.uk*
❯ The Cutting Garden, *1996*
❯ Sarah Raven's Garden Cookbook, *2007*

# WILLIAM ROBINSON
## *1838-1935*

The reputation and appraisal of William Robinson have undergone something of a revision over recent years. While his biographer proclaimed him 'unquestionably the greatest of British gardeners,'[1] the foremost historian of the Edwardian garden has characterised him as 'belligerent, cantankerous.'[2] Of course neither view need exclude the truth of the other. Certainly the range and breadth of Robinson's contribution to gardening cannot be disputed, and for those interested in the gardens of Sussex he is responsible for one of the finest – Gravetye Manor.

The details of William's background were hardly auspicious, indeed few would be surprised to find the bones of his story in the pages of a novel by Dickens. Born in County Down, Northern Ireland, in 1838, he was the eldest of three children. When William was only 10, his land agent father eloped to America with the wife of his employer. The first job the unfortunate boy was put to involved carrying pails from a river to water the plants in the glasshouses of the Marquis of Waterford. Fortunately his ambition survived undiminished and he went on to study horticulture at the National Botanic Garden in Dublin, followed by

---

**1.** *Allan, Mea,* William Robinson 1838-1935 Father of the English Flower Garden, *Faber and Faber, London, 1982, p.16.*
**2.** *Ottewill, David,* The Edwardian Garden, *Yale University Press, New Haven and London, 1989, p.6.*

employment at Ballykilcavan, where he became foreman. The Irish winter of 1860-61 was unusually severe. Legend has it that following a particularly bitter argument between the head gardener and William the latter stormed off, Dublin bound. His parting shot (allegedly) was to dampen the fires that heated the greenhouses and open all the windows, resulting in certain death for the prized and precious plants within.

A happier time awaited him at London's Royal Botanic Society gardens at Regent's Park. Here, under the tutorship of the distinguished curator Robert Marnock (see p.91), William quickly distinguished himself and gained increasing responsibility. Such was his standing that his request to visit the other botanic gardens of the UK to collect plants was enthusiastically sanctioned and financed. A long-running account of this tour appeared in the horticultural journal *The Gardeners' Chronicle* between 1863 and 1865. Thus began a writing career that was to result in 19 books, numerous articles and the editorship of several periodicals.

William left his job at the Society's gardens to become a full-time journalist and travel widely in France, Switzerland and America (he was an accomplished French linguist yet often rather confusingly advocated using English names for plants, rather than botanist's Latin). Barely a decade after the *Chronicle* articles began to appear, William launched his own magazine, *The Garden*, in 1872. He was to remain editor for 29 years, eventually handing over the role to his friend and protégé Gertrude Jekyll (see p.90). Other publications followed including *Gardening Illustrated* (which ran from 1874 to 1954) and *Farm and Home* (1882). Each was targeted at a particular readership, be they the jobbing gardener or the country house owner (with price and production values appropriately pitched). *The Garden* became a profitable vehicle for promoting his own ideas and views, while offering a stimulating mix of information, opinion and excellent writing. Whether producing books or magazines, William always strove to collaborate with the very best contemporary artists and writers (although his detractors often point out that the writers were not always fully credited).

However successful, periodicals are, by their nature, ephemeral and it is William's books that have contributed most to his enduring reputation. Undoubtedly the ones that are best remembered today are *The Wild Garden* (1871) and *The English Flower Garden* (1883). The latter is often cited as the most widely read gardening book and ran to 15 editions and numerous reprints. In his *Hardy Flowers* (1871), William introduced his notion of the 'mixed border', that combination of hardy perennial and annual plants now most commonly thought of as the herbaceous border.

This is perhaps the appropriate moment for a brief discussion on William Robinson and the notion of 'wild'. He was in the vanguard of those who vociferously raged against the 'unnatural' formality typified by the garish and regimented flower beds so popular in the Victorian era: serried ranks of equidistant blooms that were laboriously raised, bedded out, then discarded after flowering, leaving a bare patch of tilled earth awaiting its next inhabitants. Other detractors were John Ruskin and William Morris. William's interest in wild flowers arose from studying them in their native habitats, both at home and abroad. Like Jekyll he felt attracted to the subtlety and simplicity of the flowers and hardy plants he observed growing in humble cottage gardens. But neither of these discerning figures ever allowed anything approaching wild anarchy into the garden, nor did they think all formality of structure should be banished (indeed quite the reverse). Frances Wolseley (*see p. 80*) visited William at Gravetye in 1890 and later wrote to her father: 'He had a charming bit of old garden, the paths all paved. He goes in for carnations and Tea Roses chiefly.'[3] If nothing else, this comment should illustrate to the modern reader that William's notion of 'wild' and ours is rather different!

The generals and troops of the gardening world are as susceptible to periodic outbreaks of 'Battles of Styles' as any other cultural army. The contest of Natural verses Formal raged, often with great vitriol, in the latter years of the 19th century and into the 20th. Fighting in the architect's (formal) corner was Reginald Blomfield (*1856-1942*) who had published *The Formal Garden in England* in 1892, while William was his

---

3. *Wolseley, Frances,* Life and Letters, Vol. 1, *p.217, letter to her father October 5th 1890.*

worthy opponent in the opposite corner representing the gardener (natural). To briefly summarise, the architects argued that their superiority in the field of design made them best equipped to design and lay out gardens, while the gardeners felt their horticultural knowledge gave them the edge. The fight rumbled on publicly in print for some years (not always in the most gentlemanly of fashions) and William was never far from the fray.

Somewhat surprisingly, despite being the fount of so much horticultural wisdom, William at the age of 47 still had no garden of his own. But this was about to change. Financed by the proceeds of his publishing career and some astute property investments in the City, he purchased Gravetye Manor near East Grinstead in 1884. Gravetye was an Elizabethan mansion in a picturesque state of disrepair with an estate that stretched to 360 acres (146 hectares). The renovation and improvement of house and estate and the development of the extensive gardens were to become his chief occupation for the rest of his life. He bought adjoining land at a prodigious rate, increasing his holding to near on 1,000 acres (405 hectares).

Here at last William could put into practice his gardening theories and, interestingly, he was the first to admit that not all of them stood up to the test. In one of the later editions of the *The English Flower Garden* he wrote: 'Experience has taught me to throw overboard all tender plants and devote the book to hardy plants only, that may be planted in the open air on every fine day in the fall or winter.' The redesign and development of the extensive gardens at Gravetye involved a huge amount of earth moving, all achieved with men, horses and carts, driven of course by the enthusiasm and energy of William. Apart from the earth movers and diggers, William always had a team of gardeners at Gravetye; figures varying between 12 and 18 were recorded at different times. One wonders how such an army was kept on through the war years when garden labour was restricted to 'ineligibles', boys or women!

William's standards were of the highest, materials and workmanship always had to be of the best. In 1900 a lovely summer house was built in the west garden to a design by Ernest George (Harold Peto's partner, *see p.91*). Destined to become a favourite spot, it was made from stone quarried on the estate with roof beams of Gravetye oak. The house was carefully integrated with great sympathy within its rural setting, picturesque curves and gentle undulations his guiding principles. Literally thousands of bulbs, including anemones, snowdrops, daffodils, violets, fritillaries and wild tulips, were planted in the Alpine Meadow. Part of the London, Brighton and South Coast railway line ran through the Gravetye estate. William had thousands of bluebell bulbs scattered on the embankments. They still flourish each spring, hence the now restored eponymous Bluebell Railway Line. Far greater formality of layout was to be found closer to the house: 1902 had seen the implementation of a formal rose garden on the west lawn close to the manor, consisting of 46 rectangular beds, each planted with a different rose, underplanted with summer bedding. This exemplifies his penchant for formal design as opposed to formal planting, which he despised – he especially abhorred topiary.

Although contemporary accounts suggest he was often on the look out for a suitable bride, William never married. He was a vegetarian and teetotaller, cultivated, artistic and, although not always original in his thinking, was an accomplished and successful communicator of ideas – a man of immense energy and strength. Frances Wolseley (*see p.80*) described him as 'a six-foot tall, black bearded, keen-faced man' and his photographs show him as handsome and dignified well into old age. Before setting off on his daily commute to his London office, he would swim in the Lower Lake then often alight at Three Bridges station on his return journey in the evening, to sprint home to Gravetye across the fields. Consequently it can only be guessed at how he must have felt during the last 26 years of his life, confined to a wheelchair. His paralysis occurred in 1909 following a fall when walking to an evening church service at West Hoathly.

True to form, neither his gardening nor his writing stopped. Ernest Markham was employed to direct William's team of gardeners and stayed at Gravetye until his own death in 1937. William's eye was as keen as ever and he would often dislodge an aberrant weed with his walking stick while being pushed around the grounds in a wheelchair. In 1922, a specially commissioned half-track Citroën car arrived at Gravetye so William could be driven, tank-style, even to the least accessible parts of the estate. William died at home, aged 97, his energy and vigour little diminished by a long and eventful, if somewhat unexpected, life.

William chronicled much of his work at Gravetye in *Gravetye Manor or Twenty Years Work Around an Old Manor House*, published in 1911. This was to prove vital in the later restoration of the house. William left the property and land to the Forestry Commission, including the magnificent and extensive woodlands which they still manage (between 1889-90 alone he had planted 120,000 trees). But sadly the house fell into a state of disrepair until its knight in shining armour, in the guise of restaurateur Peter Herbert, leased the property in 1958. Herbert has carefully and sensitively restored William's home and it is now a much-loved country house hotel. The gardens have undergone a similar transformation and survive as a fitting tribute to their original maker.

**Top Works & Place**

❯ The Wild Garden, *1871*
❯ The English Flower Garden, *1883*
❯ *Gravetye Manor, near East Grinstead, tel. 01342 810567, website: www.gravetyemanor.co.uk*

# ARTHUR G. SOAMES
## 1854-1934

Sheffield Park Garden is undoubtedly one of the top-notch gardens in Sussex, indeed it is considered to be one of the very best woodland gardens in Britain. Covering an impressive 120 acres (49 hectares), of which almost a third is water, in autumn the colours resemble New England more than the south of England. From 1769 to 1909 the estate was home to the Earls of Sheffield. John Baker Holyroyd, the 1st Earl, commissioned the rebuilding of the house by James Wyatt in the then fashionable Gothick style and called in both Lancelot 'Capability' Brown (*see p. 86*) and Humphry Repton (*see p. 92*) to improve the grounds.

Speculation surrounds exactly what improvements Brown made as little documentation survives. In their guide book to the garden, the National Trust (the present owners) are of the opinion that his work primarily involved the felling and clearing of overgrown woodland, an opening out of the landscape, rather than the planting of new specimens. This was doubtless necessary as this site is particularly propitious for the growing of trees. Repton was later to comment: 'Such is the power of vegetation at Sheffield Place, that every berry soon becomes a bush, and every bush a tree.' Repton's work seems to have been confined to the areas closest to the house, including the creation of small lakes. The bones of what we see in the garden today was laid out by the 3rd Earl in the 19th century. He created an arboretum of exotic and native conifers and introduced many rhododendrons, azaleas and acers.

It was some of this extravagant spending on the grounds at Sheffield Park that contributed to the dire state of the 3rd Earl's financial affairs on his death in 1909. However, the gods of horticultural largesse continued to shine on Sheffied Park, this time in the shape of Arthur Gilstrap Soames. Arthur had first become enchanted with the house and grounds while staying nearby in 1889 and had asked for the first option to purchase the estate should it be for sale in the future. As well as being an interested buyer, Arthur was also one of the Earl's chief creditors so was in a strong position to negotiate, and the sale was completed in 1910.

A Lincolnshire brewer, Arthur had deep pockets and for the next 40 years lavished time, money and attention on the garden. Thousands of cartloads of loam were imported onto the site. A massive quantity of trees were planted, including the Tupelo Gum and Scarlet American Oak. This palette was further added to by Arthur's mass planting of autumn gentians, conifers, cypresses and Japanese maples. But such was Arthur's love of roses and rhododendrons that it rivalled even that for trees. The rhododendrons he planted in carefully orchestrated clumps around the lakes, while Banksian roses scrambled over the walls of the house.

Somewhat unexpectedly, at the age of 65, Arthur married for the first time. His bride was Agnes Helen Peel, granddaughter of the 19th-century prime minister, and they had two sons. Married life must have agreed with him as he was in his 80th year when he died. Agnes remained at Sheffied Park for the rest of her life. World War II was a turbulent time for the Park, with Nissen huts littering the once immaculate lawns. In 1949 Arthur's nephew, Captain Granville Soames, took over the running of the garden and put to right much of the havoc wrought by the war. Changing economic conditions forced the sale of Sheffield Park in 1953. The estate was split into lots, with house and garden sold separately. Thankfully, the National Trust acquired the garden and has continued to develop and tend it with their usual expertise and sensitivity, and of course their ownership ensures that the garden is still open to the public today.

**Top Place**

◗ *Sheffield Park, near Uckfield, tel. 01825 790231, website: www.nationaltrust.org.uk*

# SIR FREDERICK STERN
## *1884-1967*

The appellations 'war hero', 'big game hunter' and 'fearless jockey' are not often readily listed alongside that of 'gardener', yet Sir Frederick Claude Stern was as much an accomplished plantsman as a man of action. A man as much of the mind as of the world, this polymath must surely be classed as a true Sussex gardener as he transformed an unpromising site into a flourishing garden, which is still today an inspiration for all those who garden on chalk.

Frederick was the younger son of merchant banker James Julius Stern. Educated at Eton and Christ Church, Oxford, he joined the 2nd Company, London Yeomanry, The Westminster Dragoons, saw action at Gallipoli, Egypt and Palestine, was mentioned twice in dispatches and was awarded the Military Cross in 1917. A brief spell as assistant private secretary to Lloyd George followed, then alongside his banking career he continued to develop a keen interest in biology, specialising in plant cells and culture techniques. However, today Frederick Stern is best remembered for the creation of his unique garden at Highdown, outside Worthing, which was quite literally hewn from a bare chalk pit.

Highdown Towers, *c.*1820, and its accompanying land were acquired in 1909 when Frederick was in his mid-20s. He immediately began work on what was to become the garden, although he was not to take up permanent residence for a decade. He did not inherit even the skeletal bones of a garden; the only extant trees were a few oaks and beeches and the Blenheim Orange apple that still fruits on what is now the lawn of the Chalk Pit Garden. The abandoned chalk pit housed pigs and chickens in 1909 and had for many years been the repository of all household waste. In 1919 he married Sybil, and Highdown became their home for almost half a century. The expansion and development of the garden was very much a shared pleasure and passion.

This was the period when the apotheosis of gardening success and style for many was a blousy display of blooming rhododendrons, so a barren chalky site at the foot of the Downs would not have been considered serious gardening country. As he later wrote:

> No-one was able to advise us on what would grow on this nearly virgin chalk, and many discouraged us from trying anything. One eminent nurseryman when asked what to plant on the chalk cliffs, which are about 30 feet high on the north side of the pit, said nothing would grow there.[1]

Primarily a plantsman with a scientist's scholarly and empirical approach, Frederick set out on something of a crusade to prove that plants worthy of garden status could grow, and indeed thrive, on downland chalk. An advocate of the 'right plant, right place' philosophy, he tirelessly experimented with a wide variety of material from all over the globe.

Frederick subscribed to many of the great plant hunting expeditions of the day (a more appealing activity than his earlier pursuit of wild game) including Farrer's 1914 forays to Yunnan and Kansu and those of Wilson, Forrest, Kingdon-Ward and Elliott, among others. Many of the garden's magnolias, lilies, rhododendrons, azaleas and wisterias originate from stock brought back from abroad, including a Judas tree grown from seed from Afghanistan. Frederick was also responsible for many hybridisations, spending much time experimenting in his laboratory at Highdown. He developed worthy strains of several plants including iris, eremurus and daffodils (giving the varieties 'Amberley' and 'Handcross', good county names) but it was the rather neglected

---

1. Stern, Frederick, The Chalk Garden, Faber & Faber, London, 1974, p.13.

lily for which he had a real passion, and he can be credited for much of the revival of interest in this most lovely of plants, founding The Lily Group of the RHS. He also championed that unsung beauty, the tree paeony; 'Sybil Stern' was one of the many he grew and Highdown still boasts an impressive collection today. Undoubtedly one of the best-loved of Frederick's plants is the rose 'Wedding Day'. A large rambler with white fragrant blooms, it flowered for the first time on June 26th 1950, the Sterns' wedding anniversary, hence its name. *Rosa Highdownensis*, a moyesii seedling, received an RHS Award of Merit in 1958.

Frederick was an active and leading member of the horticultural world involved with the RHS, the Linnean Society and The Garden Society among others. He was awarded his knighthood in 1956 for Services to Horticulture. He published widely contributing articles to many periodicals and his books include the monographs *A Study of the Genus Paeonia*, *Garden Varieties of Galanthus* (co-authored with E.A. Bowles) and the charmingly titled *Snowdrops and Snowflakes*. However, today his most widely read book is *The Chalk Garden* (1960). It chronicles Frederick's making of the garden at Highdown and his search to find lime-loving garden-worthy plants. It is a must for the bookshelves of anyone who gardens on chalk, as indeed is a visit to Highdown.

The Sterns were welcoming hosts, always happy to share their garden with interested and enthusiastic visitors. During the 1920s and 1930s their guests included Queen Mary (who planted a hornbeam in the garden in 1920), the Duke of Windsor and Her Majesty The Queen Mother. Lady Stern survived her husband by five years but prior to her death had generously handed the garden over to Worthing Corporation (now the Borough Council). Under their careful stewardship the garden has continued to develop and thrive, despite suffering devastating losses in the Great Storm of 1987. It now houses the National Collection, *The Plant Introductions of Sir Frederick Stern*.

**Top Works & Place**

❂ The Chalk Garden, *1960*

❂ Garden Varieties of Galanthus, *(with E.A. Bowles), 1956*

❂ *Highdown Gardens, Worthing, tel. 01903 501054, website: www.highdowngardens.co.uk*

# ANGUS WHITE
*born 1949*

As soon as you pick up an *Architectural Plants* catalogue you know this is not the usual type of plant nursery (indeed they claim they are 'the antidote to garden centres'). First of all there is the production quality, then the unusual format, the fun and informative maps and plans by Paul Cox, the spot-varnished photographs that make Sussex look like the nether regions of Singapore. And finally comes the list of contents which includes: 'The Interesting Bit' (printed in red)'; 'The Useful Bit'; 'The New Bit'; 'The Boring Bit'. Then, having arrived at the nursery, if any expectations of the usual linger, a meeting with Angus White, the mover and shaker behind this emporium of exotic-looking plants, will quickly dispel them.

There is little, if anything, in Angus's background to suggest he would become this country's champion of these spiky, big-leaved, hardy evergreen beauties. Born and raised in Horsham, his early education was dominated by the sciences. He describes himself as 'an old hippie', bumming around California in the late 1960s. Retrospectively, he now thinks this time had a subliminal effect on him horticulturally, surrounded as he was by the giant North Californian Redwoods. He even befriended a palm frond, as a sort of pet, known to all as Walter! Later, in Hawaii, the ubiquitous coconut palms exerted a similar spell.

Back in England, Angus became a designer and maker of furniture. This highly skilled and practical side is key to his personality, as is his curiosity – he exudes a 'can do' approach to everything he tackles. Now married, Angus and his wife Fran began to look for somewhere to live away from London but still within reach of the capital. Finally they settled in Nuthurst, in a ruin of a house surrounded by woods and a hidden valley, with a range of outbuildings that made perfect workshops. Angus felt that here they very much had the illusion of being in deep country yet also had easy access to London and the south-east. But, unbeknown to them at the time, what was to be of more importance was their geographical proximity to several great public gardens, all in Sussex.

Angus cites the writer Alan Mitchell's observation that within a 10-mile radius of both Truro in Cornwall and Haywards Heath in Sussex can be found the greatest concentration of superb plant collections. Easily accessible from Nuthurst is Nymans, Borde Hill, Leonardslee and Wakehurst Place. Angus visited all regularly, indeed Wakehurst was vital to his horticultural education as all the plants were clearly identified. He was amazed at the variety of trees and plants but found that when he tried to buy them in nurseries and garden centres no one stocked them. More incredibly, his enquiries were met with the assertion that there was simply no demand for these wonderful specimens. 'So in a fit of pique I decided to start a nursery as no one else was growing these plants.' Thus Architectural Plants was born.

One of the first things Angus decided he needed when starting his new venture was an office. Depressed at the cabin-like structures available commercially he decided to design and build his own. Thus was created one of the iconic features of Architectural Plants, the beautiful yet incongruous Office. With its silvered timber cladding, generous verandahs and red tin roof, it is a successful marriage of disparate influences, New England meets Europe with a bit of Queensland thrown in. However, even this structure has its rival, in the shape of the elevated toilet on stilts behind, described as 'the most beautiful lavatory in Europe'. Still, back to the plants…

Angus had long bemoaned the state of his own garden through the winter months and had remedied this by creating strong architectural effects, using plants that looked good all year long. The plants were evergreen, with bold shapes; they didn't look hardy but in fact were. The scarcity of a lot of these plants was due to the fact that they were thought to be difficult to raise in our cooler, northern climes. Prior to the nursery opening in 1990 an extensive programme of propagation had begun, many of the cuttings coming from parent plants growing at the esteemed neighbouring gardens, in particular Leonardslee. Peter Tindley who formerly worked at Kew has been vital to the success of the propagation of stock. Several years on, a second Architectural Plants nursery was opened at Chichester, and now most of the plants initially raised at Nuthurst are later moved down there to grow on.

Architectural Plants is known as something of a phenomenon in the gardening world – its success and influence are marked. Perhaps no one is more surprised by this than Angus: 'I have created a market rather than spotting a demand which I then cynically filled. I admired these plants, so I thought perhaps others would too.' He freely admits he has 'something of a maverick approach to gardening' and it is interesting to note that his fellow comrades-in-arms, who began nurseries selling hardy exotics around the same time, also came from non-horticultural backgrounds. Michael Hirsch who ran Jungle Giants, now in Ludlow, had worked in animation, while Clive Shilton of Hardy Exotic Plants, in Penzance, was a former high-class shoemaker. This triumvirate was variously known as the 'new exoticists' and the 'new brutalists'.

Angus and his staff are endlessly enthusiastic about the plants they grow and always generous with advice. As the catalogue proclaims, they offer 'a list that's tailored very much for those who want to use our plants to "create an effect" – the designer, rather than the collector.' If the tone appears somewhat didactic at times, believe me, it is for your own good! Take note: 'If you want to create the sort of extraordinary exotic effects that can be created with our plants, you need to be ruthlessly uncompromising in your selection. To this end – the ones described as "ESSENTIAL" are essential!'

Perhaps not unexpectedly when asked who his gardening influences are, Angus spontaneously recites a varied list that has little to do with gardens. Least surprising was Augustus Smith, the great Victorian who created the gardens at Tresco in Cornwall, a continuing inspiration to Angus and which he describes as 'an extraordinary garden of world-class lunacy'. He goes on: 'I admire and empathise with people who have done it on their own'; these include the architect of Portmeirion, Clough Williams-Ellis, Rowena Cade whose vision created the outdoor Minack Theatre near Penzance, the geologist William 'Strata' Smith, clockmaker John Harrison, along with Isambard Kingdom Brunel and Charles Darwin – an inspiring list indeed.

Having opened the gardening world's eyes to what can be achieved using hitherto unusual hardy exotic plants and trees in British gardens, Angus now is on something of a crusade to turn our attention to 'creative maintenance', the ongoing care, assessment and editing of an ever-maturing garden. Too often customers will spend a lot of time and money implementing a new design for their garden but two years down the line the results are much less than they should be, primarily because not enough care and attention has been paid to maintaining the changing scene. This is especially true when plants are being deployed in a sculptural context. Fine adjustments must be made to any garden, however successful the initial plan. 'I wish to elevate the position of gardeners over designers', says Angus.

Part of his contribution to this end is a forthcoming venture with Chichester College (the Brinsbury Campus) where he is setting up a new nursery that will offer old-style apprenticeships so that young people can learn thoroughly the skills of propagation and maintenance. 'Presentation has always been prime to me and ongoing creative maintenance is key to this.' Certainly anyone approaching the entrance to Architectural Plants, passing the immaculate serried ranks of beautifully clipped and tended plants and trees, will know immediately what Angus White means by 'presentation'.

**Top Place**

◑ *Architectural Plants, tel. 01403 891772, website: www.architecturalplants.com*

# FRANCES WOLSELEY
## *1872-1936*

The notion that genteel and respectable women could participate in a little gentle gardening began to gain popularity in the Victorian era (in sharp contrast to the back-breaking sweeping, weeding and potato-picking undertaken by female agricultural workers). As early as the 1840s, the much-read writer Jane Loudon promoted the activity in books such as *Gardening for Ladies* and *The Ladies' Companion to the Flower Garden*. However, the idea that upper- and middle-class women might take up gardening as a profession only began to gain ground slowly. The high-profile figures Gertrude Jekyll (*see p.90*) and Ellen Willmott were both granted the RHS accolade the Victoria Medal of Honour, while the first female students appeared at Kew Gardens in 1895. Swanley and Studley Colleges soon followed offering women courses in horticulture and agriculture.

Described in her *Times* obituary as 'a great pioneer as well as a great gardener'[1], there was little in the early life of Frances Garnet Wolseley to indicate that she would be at the vanguard of this movement to promote women in horticulture. Born in Ireland in 1872, she was the only child of Garnet Joseph Wolseley and his wife Louisa. Her war hero father saw action in numerous campaigns, culminating in the failed attempt to rescue General Gordon at Khartoum. Much admired

1. Proctor, Chrystabel, 'Viscountess Wolseley Gardening For Women' obituary in The Times, December 28th 1936.

by Queen Victoria, he became a baron and later a viscount, a title inherited by his daughter on his death in 1913. Perhaps more memorably he has entered the popular imagination as 'the very model of a modern major general' in Gilbert and Sullivan's *The Pirates of Penzance* (1879).

Throughout her girlhood Frances led the nomadic life common to members of a military family which she later described as 'a very mixed life in hotels.' [2] Her familial connections also brought her the privilege of literature lessons from the poet and critic Edmund Gosse and drawing and painting lessons from the watercolourist Helen Allingham. In 1877, she was the recipient of a rather clunking tribute in the form of some McGonagall-like lines, *Impromptu to F.G.W.*, penned for her by the future poet laureate Alfred Austin.

When she was 25, her family took a 21-year lease on Farm House (now known as Trevor House), a dower house in the grounds of Glynde Place, East Sussex, and it was here that Frances, unmarried and something of an emotional slave to her beautiful but temperamental mother, could finally develop her interest in gardening. William Robinson (*see p.65*) visited and offered gardening advice shortly after they moved in.

How then did Frances move from being a dutiful daughter and amateur gardener to 'a great pioneer' who founded the Glynde College for Lady Gardeners? The story goes that Lady Wolseley saw an advertisement in the horticultural press placed by a 'lady in distressed circumstances' seeking gardening work. From this the rather unlikely scheme of taking young women as gardening students seems to have developed. At last Frances had found a cause and a channel for her energies. The start date of the school is rather hazy but certainly by early 1903 a functioning school had been firmly established in the one-acre (0.4- hectare) Farm House garden. Flowers were grown but no vegetables. Initially there were just two students and a superintendent. To extend the scope of the fledgling school's curriculum, a further acre of glebe land in the village was rented.

---

**2.** *Wolseley, Frances,* Life and Letters, Vol. 1, *p.16.*

In 1904 Gertrude Jekyll became one of the patrons of the school and she proved an enduring influence on Frances. After a visit to Jekyll's Munstead Wood garden in 1906 she wrote: 'I went to spend a night with Miss Jekyll and had the privilege of taking our then head gardener at Farm House with me. It was the day upon which I finally decided to devote the rest of my active years to garden students, so it was eventful to me.'[3] Success followed and such was the rate of expansion that Frances leased a five-and-a-half-acre (2.25-hectare) site with a workman's cottage in Glynde known as Ragged Lands. A new house (with accommodation for the superintendent, students and Frances) was erected and with the help of two local lime pit workers, a pony and a small tip cart, this windswept, chalky field was gradually transformed into a productive terraced garden. Her gardening aesthetic was influenced by trips to Italy, an effect she achieved in the English climate with hardy Irish yews and Sienese oil jars planted with box. An almost limitless supply of paying labour, in the shape of her eager young students, must also have helped to advance the garden.

The school experienced a speedy turnover of superintendents until 1916 when a former student and favourite, Elsa Russell More (1886-1933), took over. Student numbers at this time were 25. Run very much on military lines, students would report for class at 7 am dressed in sailor's hats and practical short coats and skirts. True to her army roots, Frances chose khaki for the uniform (so as not to show the chalky Sussex mud) along with stout boots, leggings and a neck tie striped with the patriotic college colours of red, white and blue. The students would don oilskins and sou'westers in 'those times of terrific, fleet-sweeping squalls'[4] and dig, plant and cultivate flowers, fruit and vegetables. During the war years (1914-16), she was characteristically to compare new students to 'the men of Kitchener's army' who, though arriving 'untidy and somewhat ungainly' were 'each week acquiring more of the upright, active, military swing'.[5]

3. Wolseley, Frances, 191 Garden Notes, 1904-09, p.53.
4. Wolseley, Frances, In a College Garden, John Murray, London, 1916, p.97.
5. Ibid., p.7.

Once Elsa More was in charge Frances was able to devote more time to outside activities. Her interests encompassed agricultural reform, fair pay for women and the revival of rural crafts. As early as 1914 she had helped found the Glynde and District Federation of Growers, a co-operative society set up to help smallholders sell their produce collectively direct at market, a worthwhile venture that sadly failed. In 1917 she took up a full-time post as organising secretary of the Women's Branch of the Board of Agriculture in East Sussex. The following year, with new colleague Mrs Molly Musgrave, she became involved in a scheme to train women smallholders. Undoubtedly, the outbreak of war, and the resulting shortage of man-power, greatly increased the impetus to involve women in the production of food, whether on the land or in the garden, and the Women's National Land Service Corps was founded. This was taken over by the government in 1917 and became the Women's Land Army. By the end of the war, 113,000 women were employed on the land.

Frances published several influential books beginning with *Gardening for Women* in 1908, followed by *In a College Garden* (1916) which chronicles the development of the school. The same year saw the publication of *Women and the Land*. Due to the wartime paper shortage, *Gardens: Their Form and Design* did not appear until 1919. However, by this time far more pressing evidence of the war had impinged on Frances and her students. The Glynde College for Lady Gardeners, situated so close to the English Channel, was touched all around by the signs of war. The surrounding Downs were darkened by 'small black masses of troops'[6] on manoeuvres. While out walking on a Sunday evening Frances heard singing voices drifting from the local church 'but all the time behind the clear village voices, there is the ceaseless boom of Flanders guns'.[7] After the war the future of the college became less certain. Frances moved into a house called Massetts Place at Scaynes Hill, East Sussex, with the now divorced Mrs Musgrave. Together they ran a smallholding and took two students, Miss McKie and Miss Reilly: 'It seemed that we

---

6. *Wolseley, Frances,* Life and Letters, Vol. 4, *p.931.*
7. *Ibid., diary entry dated August 1st 1915, p.928.*

were forming a sort of women's colony on a small scale.'[8] Tensions became evident between Frances and Elsa More, who suffered from ill health, and in the autumn of 1921 Elsa was given notice to quit Ragged Lands. After living in a cottage somewhat obscurely called 'Somewhere' on the Glynde Estate, Elsa died in 1933.

Frances continued to write, often about the history and architecture of Sussex, publishing among other titles *Some Smaller Manor Houses of Sussex* (1925) and *Some By-Ways of Sussex* (1930) along with numerous articles. In 1928 The Wolseley Room was opened at Hove Library. Here one can study Frances's books, family papers, memorabilia and her ample notes on Sussex. It is decorated with murals – *The Spirit of Agriculture* is by Gwynedd Hudson and another depicting medieval gardens is by Mary Campion (who also provided the stylish illustrations for *Gardens: Their Form and Design*). Frances Wolseley died on December 24th, 1936 at Culpeppers, Ardingly, where she had lived with Mrs Musgrove for the final ten years of her life. A memorial to her still stands in the village today, appropriately decorated with agricultural and horti-cultural icons and topped by the coronet of a viscountess.

8. *Wolseley, Frances,* Life and Letters, Vol. 4, *p.1068.*

**Top Works & Place**
- Gardening for Women, *1908*
- In a College Garden, *1916*
- *The Wolseley Room, Hove Library*

## Much more than a basket

If evidence were ever needed that Sussex is the true spiritual home of all English gardeners then surely we need look no further than that delightful item, the Sussex Trug. How many other counties can boast their very own elegant handcrafted basket for carrying all those essential gardening items, from trowels and secateurs to cut flowers and rhubarb stalks? Certainly students at the Glynde College used them.

The name trug comes from the Anglo-Saxon word 'trog', meaning a wooden vessel or boat-shaped item (think of medieval coracles and the origins of today's baskets become apparent). In the 1820s, Thomas Smith from Herstmonceux decided to develop and improve on the Anglo-Saxon original (which had been large and heavy) and invented the lightweight shallow basket we now think of as the Sussex Trug. They quickly became an indispensable item on farms and in gardens and he soon had a thriving business, operating from his home at Hormes House, Windmill Hill. He even showed his wares at the 1851 Great Exhibition in London where Queen Victoria became one of his customers.

Trugs come in varying sizes and were originally used as farm measures as well as carrying vessels. Anything from a pint of liquid to a bushel of grain feed could be measured (admittedly somewhat approximately). Still made today, the materials, tools and method used to produce a trug remain unchanged. The handles are made from coppiced sweet chestnut and the basket and feet from cricket-bat willow. Despite being light and easy to carry, they are extremely strong and hard-wearing. Indeed their longevity and reparability probably in part accounts for the sad demise of the Sussex trug maker; one trug lasts most people a lifetime. Today there are only a few skilled craftspeople left in the county making these wonderful items. Do please support them. Buy a trug today – you won't regret it!

# MORE INSPIRING SUSSEX GARDENERS

There are numerous inspiring, and sometimes very famous, gardeners who occasionally worked or lived within the county boundaries but who cannot be classed as 'Sussex gardeners'. However, such is the quality or interest of their work that I fear to omit all mention of them. Likewise, there are others who certainly deserve more than a mention but space unfortunately precludes greater detail. Here then is a brief (and certainly not exhaustive) summary of some resident and non-resident gardeners and designers (alongside others with strong horticultural links) and some of their Sussex connections.

## James Bateman
### 1812-97
A horticulturalist and botanist, Bateman was the creator of the extraordinary high Victorian garden Biddulph Grange in Staffordshire, famous for its compartments inspired by China, Egypt and Italy, and who ended his days on the Sussex coast. His particular interest was tropical plants, especially orchids, and he financed collections of the species in British Guiana, Mexico and Guatemala.

He wrote several important books on orchids and many articles. In 1884 Bateman and his wife settled in Worthing where he retired. The costly gardens at Biddulph may account for the extent of his estate at death, a meagre £273 18s 11d.

## Lancelot 'Capability' Brown
### 1716-83
Brown was the leading figure of the English landscape movement which aimed to arrange parkland, water and woodland in a seemingly 'natural' way. He undertook a huge number of commissions, was extremely influential and is considered to have been the first professional landscape designer. Brown was mostly called in to improve existing parklands by fashion-conscious aristocratic estate owners. His work in Sussex includes the parks Petworth, Cowdray, Ashburnham, Burton, Brightling, Stanstead and Sheffield.

## Priscilla Coventry
### n.d.

Known to all as 'Miss Coventry' she was the resident gardener at Folkington Place, Folkington (if you want to sound local, don't pronounce the 'lk') for a great number of years, working well past retirement age. She trained at Studley College and developed the one-and-a-half-acre (0.6-hectare) chalk garden at Folkington into a true gem. Among its admirers were Christopher Lloyd (*see p.54*) and Beth Chatto. She raised the pale yellow aquilegia 'Miss Coventry'.

## Sylvia Crowe
### 1901-97

Crowe was at the forefront of the modern movement in landscape design in the 20th century and did much to advance the profession. Her father was a fruit farmer at Felbridge, Sussex, and, due to childhood tuberculosis, Crowe spent much of her teenage years at home on the farm. The breadth of her landscape work is impressive, ranging from new towns, such as Harlow and Basildon, to nuclear power stations, hospitals, commercial buildings and large-scale projects for the Forestry Commission. In 1973 she was made a Dame of the British Empire. Her Sussex work includes a 1967 private commission for a house near Rye, advisory work for Basil Spence's

exciting new University of Sussex, 1961-69, landscape plans for the River Cuckmere, 1968, Arlington Reservoir, 1969-72 and Ardingly Reservoir in the late 1970s. It seems particularly fitting that in 1978 she was awarded an honorary degree from the University of Sussex.

## Nicholas Culpeper
### 1616-54

Culpeper was most probably born in Ockley, Surrey, where his father was rector and records of his baptism survive. However, due to the death of her husband only weeks before the birth of her son, Culpeper's mother Mary returned to live with her own family at Isfield in Sussex, where her father was rector. It was here that the young Nicholas grew up until he began his theological education at Cambridge. However, tragedy struck (quite literally) in 1634. Culpeper's lover was on her way from Sussex to meet and elope with him when she was killed by a bolt of lightning. Culpeper abandoned his studies, turned to medicine and went on to produce one of the most famous and widely read herbals of all time. Published in 1652, its full and splendid title is *The English Physitian, An astrologo-physical discourse on the vulgar herbs of this nation, being a compleat method of physik, whereby a man may preserve his body in health, or cure himself, being sick.* It is still in print today. The other Sussex connection with Culpeper is Wakehurst Place (*see p. 58*), which was his father's family seat.

## Gertrude Mary Denman
### 1884-1954

Born to privilege and wealth, Lady Denman typifies those of her class who devoted huge amounts of energy and time for the good of others. Her interests ranged widely, including wounded soldiers and sailors, professional women, land settlement and birth control. In 1916 she was elected chairman of the subcommittee of the Agricultural Organisation Society which founded the Women's Institute. The following year the W.I. was placed under the auspices of the Board of Agriculture and Fisheries, with Lady Denman becoming assistant director of the department responsible for food production by women. This experience proved invaluable in 1939 when she coordinated the re-establishment of the Women's Land Army, to provide female agricultural workers to grow much-needed food for the nation during wartime. In her typically generous style, she lent her Sussex home, Balcombe Place, to the organisation for use as its headquarters.

## Garden Schools

Apart from Frances Wolseley's Glynde College for Lady Gardeners (*see p. 80*), while writing this book, I have come across references to several other establishments in the county offering a horticultural education to women. The School of Gardening at Rye was run by the Misses Peake and Ridley; the Chapman School of Nature Study and Gardening at Clapham, near Worthing, was run by Miss Cracknell and Miss Collins; and the charmingly named Violet Nurseries could be found at Henfield.

## Fergus Garrett
### n.d.

Garrett became Head Gardener at Great Dixter in the early 1990s and developed a creative and dynamic working and personal relationship with the garden's owner Christopher Lloyd (*see p. 54*). His previous post had been at a garden in the South of France and this helped inspire his interest in tender exotic and tropical plants, many of which now contribute to what has become some of the signature planting at Dixter. Garrett and Lloyd's first joint project was the transformation of the Lutyens-designed Edwardian rose garden. This is now resplendent with dahlias, cannas, eucalyptus and banana plants throughout the summer months. Before Lloyd's death in 2006, The Great Dixter Charitable Trust was founded to ensure the survival of house and garden. A Heritage Lottery Fund Grant of £4 million was awarded to the trust in 2008. Garrett is deeply committed to and involved with the trust and has the courage and vision to take the garden into the future as a living, but not a fossilised, testament to its creator, qualities that Lloyd recognised in his friend and collaborator. Alongside his role at Dixter, Garrett is also much in demand as an inspiring and informative teacher, giving talks and demonstrations to a wide range of audiences. He also sits on several RHS committees.

## Mary Ann Gilbert
### 1776-1845

An early advocate of self-sufficiency, Gilbert owned land around Beachy Head near Eastbourne. Here she employed paupers (who she considered were demoralised and demotivated by the application of the unpopular Poor Law) to clear and improve the soil and grow potatoes. She then rented the land to these people to produce their own food. The scheme grew, as did the range of crops grown, and pigs and cows soon graced many of the new allotments. She believed the work not only put food in their bellies but also iron in their characters. The legend over the gate leading to the allotment site read: 'Here waste not Time and you'll not want Food'. By 1835 there were 213 allotment tenants on this most bracing of sites and in the following decade she founded two agricultural schools for her tenants' children to attend (at Willingdon and East Dean).

## The Greengage

In case any Sussex inhabitants are tempted to plant plum trees as a patriotic act, I feel a brief mention of the greengage should be made in an attempt to correct a much propounded misapprehension. It is often cited that this tasty plum was introduced into England by the Gage family at Firle. However, current thinking supports the theory that the first French 'Reine Claude' plum trees to arrive in England were actually destined for Sir Thomas Gage's residence at Hengrave Hall, Suffolk – nowhere near Sussex. En route from France, the labels became detached from the trees and Sir Thomas's gardener relabelled them 'Green Gage'. Similarly the popular 'Victoria' plum is said to be a chance seedling originally found in a garden at Alderton in Sussex, yet no such village exists in the county. Such is the stuff that myths are made of! If you do want to plant fruits of true Sussex origins then choose one of the county's many apples (*see p. 31*).

## Frederick Hanbury
### 1851-1938

The Hanbury Herbarium was Hanbury's assembly of 12,000 wild European plants collected throughout the 19th century, which he donated to the RHS in 1936. A resident of Sussex, he bought the Brockhurst Park estate, near East Grinstead, in 1908. His substantial finances enabled him to develop the grounds, establishing a spectacular Rock Garden, Pinetum and Wilderness with the assistance of 40 gardeners. Among the plants that furnished the Rock Garden were quantities from his cousin Thomas Hanbury's French garden, La Mortola.

## Gertrude Jekyll
### 1843-1932

The famous author and garden designer is most readily associated with her beloved home county of Surrey, yet she is responsible for garden plans not only all over the British Isles but also on the Continent and in the United States. (She rarely visited sites but provided detailed plans based on descriptions and measurements of individual locations.) Unfortunately, Sussex is not rich in Jekyll gardens. Perhaps the best known is the King Edward VII Sanatorium at Midhurst, the 1906 purpose-built hospital for the treatment of tuberculosis and consumptive diseases. Jekyll provided plans for the grounds and supplied plants from her nursery. Frances Wolseley's students from the Glynde College for Lady Gardeners (*see p.80*) implemented her plans. Some fascinating photographs document the students at work. During the 1880s she created the garden of her great friend the early feminist Barbara Bodichon's cottage at Scarlands Gate, Hardings Wood, near Robertsbridge. She also did work at West Dean Park, Arundel Castle, Buckhurst Park, Barton St Mary, Frant Court, Little Thakenham and Plumpton Place, and undertook some smaller domestic commissions, such as The Hoo at Willingdon, near Eastbourne.

## Charles Eamer Kempe
### 1837-1907

Kempe was an architect and noted ecclesiastical designer and many Sussex churches contain examples of his stained glass. The garden of his home, Old Place at Lindfield, he developed in the Arts and Crafts style, full of visionary vistas and axes delineated by tall yew hedges. Gertrude Jekyll was a friend, so may have been involved with the garden's layout, if only informally. Frances Wolseley (*see p.80*) also recorded visits to Old Place with her mother.

### Sir Edwin Landseer Lutyens
### 1869-1944

The Arts and Crafts architect designed many influential gardens in this country and abroad. Lutyens often worked with Gertrude Jekyll (*see p.90*), and each favoured linking their gardens closely to the architectural context of the house, using the same palette of building materials for garden structures such as steps and terraces. In collaboration with Jekyll he worked at Little Thakenham, The Hoo at Willingdon and Plumpton Place. Other Sussex commissions include Buckhurst Park and, of course, the work he did for Nathaniel Lloyd (*see p.54*) at Great Dixter.

### Robert Marnock
### 1800-89

Distinguished Scottish garden designer and horticulturalist, Marnock was tutor to William Robinson (*see p.65*) while curator of the Royal Botanic Society's garden at Regent's Park, London. In the 1870s, Hastings Borough Council commissioned him to carry out extensive work on the town's Alexandra Park. He extended the botanical interest of the planting, adding interesting exotics and a wide variety of trees. He also worked on Dunorlan Park, in Tunbridge Wells, just over the border in Kent.

### Harold Ainsworth Peto
### 1854-1933

Originally trained as an architect, Peto worked for many years in a successful partnership with Ernest George, but later concentrated on his real interests of interior and garden design. At West Dean Gardens (*see p.24*) he was responsible for the fabulous 328-foot (100-metre) long stone and flint pergola constructed in 1910. At Sedgwick Park, George and Peto were commissioned to make additions and changes to the house in 1886, with more work done in 1903 and 1904. The gardens at Sedgwick are typical of Peto, though no documentary evidence of his work there survives.

### Sir Henry & Lady Eve Price
### n.d.

The Prices bought Wakehurst Place (*see p.58*) in 1936 and continued the development of the gardens begun by Sir Gerald Loder. Under Lady Eve the gardens became regular exhibitors at the RHS shows and the award-winning plants *Viburnum* 'Eve Price' and *Pieris* 'Henry Price' were named after them. It was due to the Prices' generosity that the estate was bequeathed to the National Trust in 1963.

## Humphry Repton
### 1752-1818

Repton was the next big name on the landscape scene after Lancelot 'Capability' Brown. He continued many of his predecessor's ideas concerning the design of parkland but also incorporated flower beds close to the house, often quite formal in design. Part of his legacy is his wonderful series of *Red Books* which he prepared for clients. Each contains a series of watercolours which show the landscape both before and (once the flap is lifted) after the proposed improvements. He worked widely across the county including drawing up plans for the Royal Pavilion at Brighton. Other Sussex sites associated with Repton are the parks Brightling, Buckhurst, Kidbrooke, Sheffield and Uppark.

## Seedy Sunday

No one individual is behind my next listing, rather it is the enthusiasm and dedication of a small team of committed volunteers who make this worthwhile event happen. Since 2001, Seedy Sunday has taken place in Brighton and Hove every February (*see www.seedysunday.org* for more details). It is now the UK's biggest seed swap devoted to preserving and spreading traditional varieties of open-pollinated 'heritage' flowers, fruit and vegetables among amateur growers.

No longer commercially available, the demise of these threatened varieties may represent a real danger to the future security of food production so it is vital that they continue to be grown. As their website states, the annual event unites 'gardeners, seed savers, herb and wild flower enthusiasts, local garden and community groups as well as organisations and campaigners for sustainable food production and biodiversity'. However, don't let this put you off as it also looks jolly good fun and a great day out for anyone interested in growing even just a few strange or unusual varieties of tomatoes. Sponsored by Brighton's Infinity Foods it also boasts a great organic café.

## Tony Schilling
### n.d.

Schilling oversaw the gardens at Wakehurst Place (*see p.58*) from 1969-91 and the Asian Heath Garden is named in his honour. As a plant collector with a particular penchant for Himalayan plants, especially rhododendrons, Wakehurst was the perfect environment for Schilling. He also designed the Himalayan Glade. His introductions include *Euphorbia schillingii*, *Skimmia laureola* and *Populus glauca*.

**Colonel Robert Stephenson Clarke**
**1862-1948**

Clarke purchased the Borde Hill estate near Haywards Heath in 1893. He was a keen naturalist and patronised many of the great plant hunters of the period: Farrer, Forrest, Kingdon-Ward, Rock and Wilson introductions are all represented in the plant stock at Borde Hill. At one time, 27 full-time gardeners tended the site. Rhododendrons, azaleas and camellias all flourish here. Borde Hill is still owned and run by Clarke's descendants who continue his excellent work.

**Andy Sturgeon**
**n.d.**

Sturgeon is among the generation of new, innovative garden designers who have become widely known to the public through their appearances on television and through books and magazines. He runs a successful garden design practice in Brighton, producing a wide range of designs for corporate and private clients. His work often incorporates sculpture and lighting, something that is too often neglected in the garden. He has won three RHS Gold Medals at the Chelsea Flower Show as well as awards at the Hampton Court Flower Show and from the British Association of Landscape Industries.

**Christopher Tunnard**
**1910-79**

Canadian by birth, Tunnard was a leading pioneer of the modernist movement who designed the garden at Bentley Wood, Halland. Serge Chermayeff (architect, in collaboration with Erich Mendelssohn, of the county's ultimate modernist icon, the De La Warr Pavilion at Bexhill) designed and built Bentley Wood for himself in the late 1930s. Set amid an open landscape of trees and grass, flowers were few, limited primarily to drifts of spring bulbs, while exotic blooms flowered alongside the house. Tunnard's original layout included the careful positioning of a sculpture by Henry Moore. Sadly, due to Chermayeff's bankruptcy, Moore's *Recumbent Figure* is now long gone.

# INDEX

**A**gapanthus     *42*
apples     *31-2*
Architectural Plants     *77-9*
Austin, Alfred     *81*

**B**arrow Hill     *17-18*
Bateman, James     *86*
Bateman's     *9, 50-3*
Bell, Vanessa     *12-16*
Bentham, George     *19*
Bentley Wood     *93*
Birley, Sir Oswald     *37*
Birley, Lady Rhoda     *37*
Blomfield, Reginald     *38, 67-8*
Bloomsbury Group     *12, 16*
Bluebell Railway Line     *69*
Bodichon, Barbara     *90*
Bolt, Grace 'Gay'     *45-6*
Borde Hill     *93*
Borrer, William     *9, 11, 17-19*
Brighton Parks     *33-5*
Brockhurst Park     *90*
Bromfield, Rev. William A.     *19*
Brookes, John     *20-3*
Brown, Lancelot 'Capability'     *71, 86*
Buckland, Jim     *24-7*
'The Bungalow'     *29-30*

**C**ampion, Mary     *84*
Charleston Farmhouse     *9, 12-14*

Charleston Manor     *37*
Chermayeff, Serge     *93*
Chichester College     *79*
Clarke, Colonel Robert     *93*
Coates, Alfred     *59-60*
Cockerell, Olive J.     *9, 28-31, 32*
Colvin, Brenda     *20*
Conran, Terence     *21*
Coventry, Priscilla     *87*
Cox, Paul     *76*
Crowe, Sylvia     *20, 87*
Culpeper, Nicholas     *87-8*

**D**arby, Dr Lewis     *32*
Dedman, William     *15*
Denman, Gertrude Mary     *88*
Denmans Garden     *20*
Dodson, Harry     *25*
Don, Monty     *63*

**E**gremont, Lord     *31*
The Elms     *50*
Erodium     *42*
Evison, J.R.B.     *23, 33-5*

**F**arm House     *81-3*
Folkington Place     *87*
Ford, Sidney     *32*
Fry, Roger     *13*

| | | | |
|---|---|---|---|
| **G**age, Sir Thomas | 89 | Johnston, Lawrence | 12 |
| Garden Schools | 88 | | |
| Garnett, David | 13 | **K**empe, Charles Eamer | 90 |
| Garrett, Fergus | 57, 88-9 | King Edward VII Sanatorium | 90 |
| George, Ernest | 69, 91 | Kipling, Carrie | 50, 52-3 |
| Gilbert, Mary Ann | 89 | Kipling, Rudyard | 50-3 |
| Glynde | 39-40, 81-4 | Kreutsberger, Sibylle | 40, 41 |
| Godfrey, Walter H. | 36-8 | | |
| Goffin, Lucy | 40-1 | **L**atham, Sir Paul | 37 |
| Gough, Graham | 39-42 | Leonardslee | 32, 58, 60-1, 78 |
| Grant, Duncan | 13-14 | Lithodora | 42 |
| Gravetye Manor | 32, 65, 67, 68-70 | Lloyd, Christopher | 6, 23, 41, |
| Gray, Rose | 64 | | 54-7, 63, 88 |
| Great Dixter | 40, 54-7, 62, 88-9 | Lloyd, Daisy | 54, 55 |
| greengages | 89 | Lloyd, Nathaniel | 23, 51, 54-7 |
| | | Loder, Sir Edmund | 60, 61 |
| **H**anbury, Frederick | 90 | Loder, Sir Gerald | 23, 58-61 |
| Hellyer, Arthur | 9, 23, 43-6 | Loder, Sir Giles | 23, 60-1 |
| Hemerocallis | 42 | Loder, Reginald | 60 |
| herbariums | 19 | Loder, Sir Robert | 58 |
| Herbert, Peter | 70 | Loudon, Jane | 80 |
| Herstmonceaux Castle | 37 | Lutyens, Sir Edwin | 54-5, 91 |
| The High Beeches | 58 | | |
| Highdown | 73-5 | **M**annington, John | 32 |
| Hill, Octavia | 8 | Marchants Hardy Plants | 39, 40-2 |
| Hirsch, Michael | 78 | Markham, Ernest | 69 |
| Hogg, Robert | 32 | Marnock, Robert | 66, 91 |
| Holyroyd, John Baker | 71 | Middle Farm Shop | 32 |
| Hooker, Sir William | 19 | Millennium Seed Bank | 60 |
| Hudson, Gwynedd | 84 | Mitchell, Alan | 77 |
| Hussey, Christopher | 37 | Monk's House | 12, 14-16 |
| | | More, Elsa Russell | 82-3, 84 |
| **J**arman, Derek | 12, 47-9 | Musgrave, Molly | 83, 84 |
| Jekyll, Gertrude | 56, 66, 67, | | |
| | 80, 82, 90, 91 | **N**icolson, Adam | 63, 64 |
| John, C.A. | 52 | Nussey, Helen | 9, 28-31, 32 |
| Johnson, G.C. | 34 | | |

Old Place 90
Orchards (Rowfant) 45-6

Parsons, Trekkie 16
Pearl, R.T. 34
Peel, Agnes Helen 72
Perch Hill 63-4
Peto, Harold Ainsworth 91
Pickard-Smith, Katie 39-40
plums 89
Preston Park 34
Price, Lady Eve 60, 91
Price, Sir Henry 60, 91
Princep, H.C. 32
Prospect Cottage 47-9
Ragged Lands 82, 84
Raven, Sarah 62-4
Repton, Humphrey 71, 92
rhododendrons 61
Robinson, Joyce 20
Robinson, William 32, 38, 52, 55, 65-70, 81, 91

Sackville-West, Vita 12, 13, 64
Schilling, Tony 92
Schwerdt, Pam 40, 41
Sedgwick Park 91
Sedum 42
Seedy Sunday 92
Sheffield Park Garden 71-2
Shepheard, Sir Peter 14
Shepherd, Mr 31
Shilton, Clive 78
Simpson, Mr 32
Sissinghurst 40, 64
Smith, Augustus 78-9
Smith, Thomas 85

Soames, Arthur G. 71-2
Soames, Captain Granville 72
Sooley, Howard 49
Spry, Constance 64
Stern, Sir Frederick 6, 11, 23, 73-5
Stern, Sybil 74, 75
Strangman, Elizabeth 40, 48
Streeter, Fred 32
Sturgeon, Andy 93

Thoday, Peter 25
Tindley, Peter 78
Trevor House 81
trugs 85
Tunnard, Christopher 93
Turley, Mr 32

Victoria Medal of Honour 23, 35, 46, 56, 60, 61, 80

Wain, Sarah 24-7
Wakehurst Place 58-61, 77, 88, 91, 92
Washfield Nursery 40, 48
West Dean Gardens 24-7, 32, 91
White, Angus 76-9
Whittier, J.G. 59
Willmott, Ellen 80
Wolseley, Frances 9, 52-3, 67, 69, 80-5, 90
Wolseley, Garnet Joseph 80-1
Woolf, Leonard 12-16
Woolf, Virginia 13, 14-15, 16
Wratten, Edmund 36
Wyatt, James 71